# MORE THAN FIFTY PERCENT

## Woman's Life in a Newfoundland Outport
## 1900–1950
## by

HILDA CHAULK MURRAY

BREAKWATER BOOKS LIMITED

*To the memory of my parents*
*Christopher and Deborah Chaulk*
*and my Aunt Hilda*

MEMORIAL UNIVERSITY OF NEWFOUNDLAND FOLKLORE
AND LANGUAGE PUBLICATIONS MONOGRAPH SERIES
No. 2, 1978

General Editor, Herbert Halpert

CANADA'S ATLANTIC FOLKLORE AND FOLKLIFE SERIES NO. 3, 1979

Consulting Editor, Kenneth S. Goldstein

Canadian Cataloguing in Publication Data

Murray, Hilda.
  More than 50%

(Atlantic Canada's folklore and folklife series ; 3
ISSN 0708-4226)

Bibliography: p.
ISBN 0-919948-74-X

1. Murray, Hilda.    2. Women – Newfoundland –
Biography.    I. Title.    II. Series.

FC2176.1.M87A3    971.8′04′0924    C79-094626-2
F1123.M87A3

# Contents

# Acknowledgments

First of all I wish to thank my friends in Elliston, Trinity Bay, whose memories make up such a large part of this book, and who, by their whole-hearted participation, made my fieldwork an interesting and enjoyable experience: Mr. and Mrs. Edwin Baker; Mr. and Mrs. Edward (Flora) Chaulk; Mr. and Mrs. Noah (Sarah) Chaulk: Mr. and Mrs. Robert (Annle) Chaulk; Mrs. Elizabeth (Betsy) Crewe; (Mrs.) Esther Crewe; Mr. and Mrs. William (Orpah) Crewe; Mr. and Mrs. Josiah (Maude) Hobbs: Mr. and Mrs. Aubrey (Jane) Pearce; Mr. and Mrs. Frederick (Rhoda) Pearce; Miss Lily Pearce; (Mrs.) Nina Pearce; (Mrs.) Hilda Porter; (Mrs.) Mary Jane Porter; (Mrs.) Emily Tilley; Mr. and Mrs. Charles (Blanche) Trask; (Mrs.) Violet Trask. Special thanks are due to my paternal aunt, the late (Mrs.) Hilda Porter, who was not only my chief informant but also checked the authenticity of my material.

When I was preparing this study as my Master's thesis in Folklore at Memorial University of Newfoundland, I discussed various topics with my fellow graduate students and with Mrs. G.F. (Winnie) Martin. (Mrs.) Violetta M. Halpert, Dr. David J. Hufford, Dr. J.D.A. Widdowson, and Dr. W.J. Kirwin suggested helpful material. (Mrs.) Joan Halley of the Newfoundland Dictionary Centre assisted me on dialect words. Dr. N.V. Rosenberg read the rough draft of my study and made suggestions for its inprovement. (Mrs.) Pamela Kipnis typed the final thesis. I thank them all for their help.

For assistance in transforming the academic thesis into book form, I extend my thanks to Violetta M. Halpert, who made valuable suggestions on the reorganization and tightening of the manuscript; to Pamela J. Gray, who did the preliminary technical editing; to Martin Lovelace, who was responsible for most of the final editing; and to (Mrs.) Magda Moyes, who typed the final manuscript as well as some earlier revisions. Support for the final editing and typing came from a Canada Council Grant to Professor Halpert for Newfoundland folklore publications.

My greatest debt is to Dr. Herbert Halpert, for his scholarly advice, encouragement, and patience through all the stages of my work. My thesis was written under his direction, and it was he who insisted that I should revise it for publication, and who elicited additional material and further insights during our conferences. To the editing of the revised version he contributed judicious attention to detail and experienced editorial judgment. Words fail to express my gratitude for all his help and support.

# Introduction

I was born at the height of the Depression in the fishing community of Elliston at the tip of the Bonavista Peninsula on the east coast of Newfoundland. As a child I knew Elliston as a thriving community with everyone busy — men, women, and children. Today, its one industry, the inshore fishery, is almost defunct and the community seems to be made up chiefly of retired people on pensions or people who are unemployed. I was a teenager at the time of Confederation with Canada in 1949 and was fiercely anti-Canadian. Even today I tend to think of myself as a Newfoundlander first and a Canadian second. Perhaps my attitude is a bit more understandable when one realizes that in Elliston our contacts with mainland Canada before 1949 were few indeed. Canadian goods coming into the Dominion of Newfoundland before Confederation were subject to duties. Hardly anyone from the community went to the mainland to work; the great exodus to Toronto had not yet begun. We felt closer to the United States. Nearly every family in Elliston had several relatives living somewhere in the United States, chiefly around Boston. Most of them had emigrated during the 1920s, though many had gone earlier. During the Second World War the community had come to know some Americans when a small "listening post" military base was established at "Mark's Path" in Elliston. The American boys got on well with the people of the community. The doctor from the base worked closely with the medical staff of the Bonavista Cottage Hospital and was very obliging to the local people. Towards the end of the war the base came under Canadian control and was run quite differently. People found the Canadian soldiers stuffy and cold in comparison to the easy-going American boys. I was too young to have any ideas on the subject but this was the attitude that filtered down to me from my elders.

Like most of my contemporaries in Elliston, after completing high school I left the community and have returned to it only for short intervals, usually in the summertime. The intervening years since 1950 have been spent mainly in the urban areas of Newfoundland except for one year of teaching on the west coast of the island. I was at Memorial University in St. John's for the period 1950–1954 and most of my teaching has been done in and around that city; but, I also spent four years teaching at Gander in central Newfoundland.

The fishery was still very important in Elliston during the 1950s, but towards the end of the decade it became evident that it was dying out. Fewer crews took part in the fishery each year. Where once there were upwards of one hundred boats "on the collar" (moored or anchored in a safe area some distance from the shore) during the fishing season, now there are but three. A way of life has gone forever — a life of which I was once a part. Children growing up in Elliston today are quite unaware of conditions that existed just a few short years ago.

I was conscious of the great changes taking place in Elliston in recent years, but I did not become especially interested in studying the old ways until I decided to take courses in the Department of Folklore at Memorial University in 1969. Undoubtedly my interest in folklore sprang from my strongly nationalistic and regionalistic feelings. I was intrigued by the chance to study my own culture, particularly since it was changing so much in my lifetime.

During my first year of graduate study, 1969–1970, I attended classes in the introductory course in folklore, folksong, folklife and Newfoundland history. All of these played a part in preparing me for my field work carried out during the summer of 1970. Weekly collecting for Dr. Halpert's introductory class made me aware of the vast amount and variety of folklore to be found in Newfoundland. In this course concentration was chiefly on different aspects of our own tradition. Obtaining material for a paper on death and funeral practices involved collecting with pen and notebook from people I knew. For a paper on fishing boats I went further afield and interviewed strangers. A paper on the history of Elliston enriched my knowledge of its background and heightened my interest in the community.

In the various papers I wrote for my folklore classes I found myself stressing women's activities, but found little on this in published collections. Folklorists seemed intent merely on recording texts, and the woman's importance in traditional life received only passing attention. I found books by anthropologists concerning "growing up" and "woman's role" in other cultures valuable because I was made aware of the differences that existed between those cultures and mine. Autobiographical books dealing with rural areas in Britain and the United States provided parallels which made me remember things from my childhood that I might otherwise have forgotten. I have drawn attention to some of these parallels through the numbered footnotes which appear at the end of the book. I believe many Newfoundlanders will be interested to learn, as I was, that some of the traditions which we assume originated in Newfoundland are part of the broader English tradition carried to the New World.

I thought the role women played in a fishing community was a topic worthy of study, and I was certain that in my own community I could easily collect this material so frequently overlooked by folklorists. With the knowledge that this would be an acceptable topic for my master's thesis, I began my summer field work in Elliston in 1970.

I did not have to explain my interest in folklore to the people of Elliston. They knew my parents, and my upbringing. They knew my father's fondness for a funny story and a joke, my mother's knowledge of family relationships and community history, and her special attention to the celebration of birthdays, anniversaries, etc. Hardly a day passed in our house when we were children but some member of the family would give at least the punchline of one of Father's oft-told anecdotes, applying it to the situation at hand. Invariably, the result would be delighted laughter from nearly everyone else. Or, Mother would comment that it was so-and-so's birthday; she knew the birthdate of practically everyone around, not just the members of our immediate family.

For years my mother kept a diary. During my childhood this was simply a lined exercise book. Here she noted the births, deaths and marriages in the community, unusual weather conditions, any special visitors, and events of note in the community and in the world at large. She rarely knew the direction of the wind so her invariable question to Father when she was writing up the day's events was, "How's the wind today, Chris?" Many people were aware of her fondness for recording events and one of my neighbours during the summer of 1970 asked me to check my mother's diary to see when her father had died. She herself wasn't certain of the date, but she added: "If anyone has it written down, your mother has."

My mother also had a great respect and fondness for things that were handed down in the family. Often I was told as a child where this or that piece of glassware came from, how, and why. There were scraps of family history, and incidents (often humorous) from the past. For example, we were told of when her paternal grandfather went to collect his bride-to-be from Tickle Cove, Bonavista Bay. In those days of sailing ships she had no prior notice of his coming and he found her busy harvesting potatoes. "She had to go aboard his schooner from the pratie garden."

Mother read to us and encouraged us to read. Before we could read for ourselves, hardly a winter Sunday afternoon passed without her reading some book or long magazine story to us — mystery, adventure, love, western, murder — whatever might be available. Her audience consisted of her own three children, plus two or three boys from the neighbourhood. She would be permitted to stop for supper only, and then she would finish the story by lamplight. Sometimes it would be nearly midnight when she ceased reading.

Since people in Elliston knew my background, they thought it only natural for me to carry on my mother's tradition and record the ways I knew in my youth. It was a tremendous advantage to be collecting in my home community. I am firmly convinced that any success I have had in collecting and the ease with which the material was elicited was due in no small measure to my family and my parents. They had kept the kind of home from which no traveller, friend or stranger, was permitted to leave without a meal — a cup of tea, if he'd have no more.

Because Maberly, the section of Elliston which is home to me, lay at the road's end and there was no public eating establishment near at hand, Mother felt it her duty to have any traveller — salesman, oilman, tourist — in for a meal if he happened on her doorstep around mealtime. She never expected or ever got material rewards for her kindness except on one occasion when an old gentleman, a stranger, found himself in Maberly at dinnertime. He insisted on paying for his meal but Mother would have none of it. After he had gone she discovered a fifty-cent piece pushed under his plate. She kept it for years afterward!

Father, too, believed in dispensing hospitality to others, especially travellers. Once, during the early years of his marriage, he was on his way to the woods for a load of boughs (used for kindling fires in summer), when he met an acquaintance from Little Catalina who had been searching for his horse all day. (Horses not used during the summer were let feee to roam the countryside). He made the man promise that he would call at the house for a cup of tea. Then, just in case the man might not do so, he turned round and brought him home for a meal. I regard this action as a case of truly "casting one's bread upon the waters". Although the results of this act of kindness were not forthcoming in my parents' lifetimes, I benefited from it. For the man who sought the horse back in the early 1930s was my chief non-Elliston informant for my folklife paper. Apparently his wife was rather unwilling that he become involved for fear that I would "laugh at his way of putting things down." However, he said he'd chance that; seeing whose daughter I was I couldn't be too bad. He told me of his misgivings and also his reasons for helping me when I called on him at his home during the summer of 1970 to express my thanks in person.

With the advantages of my background and knowledge of the community and with some confidence in my field work ability, I looked forward to the official beginning of my research. There was only one area about which I had some uncertainty. Although I had used a tape recorder occasionally, I still wasn't at ease with it. But somehow I overcame this because the tape recorder was in constant use whenever I was interviewing.

I explained my use of the tape recorder to the people I visited by saying that I wanted to preserve the information that they could give me about the past so that I could refer to it later for my university work. None of the Elliston people voiced any suspicions about why I was collecting information about the past. Only once did I run into a person, the daughter of a very knowledgeable couple, who was rather critical until she learned my identity and heard my motives for collecting. Once she realized I wasn't just a slick operator trying to take advantage of trusting people, she could not have been nicer to me.

I must confess, however, that I approached every collecting session with new people with some trepidation, fearful of my reception. Usually on my first visit I went by car, and would leave the tape recorder in the car until I had explained to the people of the house my reason for presenting myself so unexpectedly on their doorstep. My reception was always so friendly that on future trips I could walk in with my equipment. I found when I had two or three people in a room that after I got them started on a topic I hardly needed to direct the questioning at all. Often they would keep the conversation going in the direction I wanted without any help from me.

Since I was trying to reconstruct the pattern of life of the past I could not rely on any one person's memory alone. I asked the same questions again and again of different people. Usually I found that each of the answers backed up the others and the whole provided a fuller picture.

The quality of my tape recordings varies, for I took each situation as I found it. One could not always follow instructions about ideal recording situations. I was not about to tell a man in his eighties that the tapping of his matchbox on the table made a very annoying sound on the tape. I recorded his relaxed conversation and worried about the noise later. All sorts of noises found their way onto my tapes; the ticking and striking of clocks, the squeaking of rockers, the clanking of stove lids, the howling of the wind, the crying of children, the sounds of television programmes and background conversations, and the ringing of telephones. The latter sound I found the most annoying and difficult to eliminate entirely from the tape, for in Maberly and the Neck, ten households were on the same line. Five telephones would ring until the correct party answered. Oftentimes an interesting point was drowned out by the ringing. However, the sneakiest of all noises that I encountered in the kitchens, where most of my collecting took place, was the sound of a kettle boiling. I had no idea at the time that it would do such a thorough job of blotting out conversation, but it was quite as effective as the known enemy, the noisy phone.

Collecting information about most aspects of the old way of life was almost absurdly easy. People seemed pleased to talk about how to make blubber soap, how to treat wool from the shearing to the wearing, what the older houses were like, cures and charms, customary foods and clothing.[1]

Because I was interested in the total picture of everyday things of the past, I had an advantage over collectors who limit themselves to specific genres like folksongs or folktales. People were not being called upon to perform. They were only talking naturally with me in a familiar conversational situation on topics of mutual interest. Hence the problem of freezing-up, or artificiality, did not arise. Such tales as I collected were told as part of the conversation.

As a local person I not only had an inside track but also the added advantage of talking about things which were familiar to me. Were I an outsider some people might have tried to pull my leg — a not-unknown practice for Newfoundlanders when dealing with outsiders. I could speak their language even though I had not used some of the words and expressions since my high school days. In Newfoundland and probably elsewhere as well, when people talk of things interesting to them they talk rapidly in their local speech, to the dismay of strangers. I had no trouble understanding perfectly what they said at the time, though I must confess that later it was not quite so easy to transcribe such sessions. Luckily only one or two tapes presented any serious transcription problems. A stranger to the dialect would, I am sure, find these particular tapes indecipherable.

Unlike an outsider, I did not have to spend time choosing a place to live. Naturally, if I were spending any time in the area I was expected to live in my old home, so there I stayed. Often people told me how pleased they were to see the lights "blooming" from the windows once more. And, one night, about 10:00 p.m., we were visited by two women, married now and living on the North Side, but former residents of Maberly. As young girls they had often come to our house with their knitting during the long winter nights. As they were passing by that evening, they saw the lights, remembered past visits, and came in.

Obviously my collecting in Elliston could not have been done on a nine-to-five routine. No housewife, however friendly, wanted to see me in the morning hours when she was busy with her housework and was listening to one of the "open line" shows on the radio. At that time I would have been an unwelcome interruption. Besides, my family also needed attention.

Whether I collected in the afternoon or not depended on the weather. If it was wet and miserable, I tried to set off between 2:30–3:00 p.m. I could be fairly sure that my informants would be at home and welcome a visit. On the other hand, I did not feel like trapping my informants indoors on a sunny summer afternoon. On such afternoons our family, like many others, headed for the beach at Sandy Cove, a mile away, where I renewed contacts with people I had not met for years and all of us enjoyed the sun and the sea.

I truly enjoyed my field collecting. Meeting people I had not really talked to for years was an unexpected pleasure, perhaps because I have always liked to chat with older people. Older men as well as women gave me information; the men were as knowledgeable as the women on many aspects of the "woman's role" and as willing to talk about it. Often when I was interviewing an elderly couple the husband supplemented the wife's account. The men were well aware of the importance of the woman's contribution. It was a man who declared: "Women did more than half the work." And another said: "It couldn't have been done without the women."

My informants recognized that a way of life had gone forever and the knowledge would be irretrievably lost unless they helped me record it.

The life pattern that I experienced as a child was only slightly different from that of my parents' generation. That of today's child, whether living in Elliston or some other corner of Canada, is quite different. Children in my day were somewhat in awe of older peoples' knowledge. Today's children have lost this feeling, and even when grandparents are at hand, think their ways are too old-fashioned to bother with. It is less likely that sayings and traditions will be passed from grandparents to today's children.

People in their seventies and eighties see members of my age group as still having common ties with them, even though we also belong to the changing present. For them we are a bridge, as it were, between two worlds. Because I was "one of them", a local girl, childhood friend of their sons and daughters, they knew I was asking questions in order to fill out gaps in my own knowledge of what things used to be like. I was not a foreigner or outsider who might be suspected of wanting to show the rest of the world how quaint we used to be or still are. My informants were at ease with me at all times. Why should they feel otherwise? I was a known quantity. And, because of fairly frequent visits home over the years, many of them had become acquainted with my husband and, more recently, my children.

My twenty-three informants, were, I believe, fairly representative members of the community. They ranged in age from the middle forties to the eighties, with most of the information coming from couples in their seventies and eighties. I also received valuable material from a woman in her forties and another in her sixties; the latter was particularly good because she had grown up in a household where stories, jokes, and tricks were the rule. Some of the people I talked to were parents of large families; others had reared only one or two children. They were from varying religious backgrounds, Anglican, United Church, Salvation Army, the three denominations in the community during the period 1900–1950.

My paternal aunt, Hilda (Chaulk) Porter, was my staunch supporter and invaluable aid. Not only was she one of by best informants but she also helped me with some of my interviews. On several occasions I held my interviewing sessions at her house and she elicited material which I might have overlooked. Once she took me to visit an elderly couple, Mr. and Mrs. Charles Trask, distant relatives who live on the North Side of Elliston. On this occasion she did most of the questioning, showing that she clearly understood what I was after.

Obviously considerable variations exist even in such a small community. Of the four sections of Elliston I worked in three: Maberly, Neck and Elliston Centre. I wish now that I had ranged further afield. Looking back I wonder if it was lack of time or the fact that they were strangers which caused me to neglect the people of the North Side.

The people I talked with felt the need to preserve the knowledge of what it was like "years ago." Many were proud of having passed through the tough depression years, and though all agreed it was a life of back-breaking toil, "one drop of sweat pushin' the other, maid," they admitted that they had enjoyed the hustle and bustle of life then. One couple, in their eighties now, said if they had to relive their lives they would not want to change anything about them.

Sometimes I felt guilty about taking so much and seemingly giving nothing in return. But looking back on those summer visits I realize my informants too enjoyed those chats. For one thing they had the pleasure of reliving the active part of their careers. For another, as I mentioned earlier, they recognized they were helping me to record a way of life that had disappeared. Perhaps some day their grandchildren will be grateful that we worked together to record the traditions they were not at hand to learn for themselves.

H.C.M.

# Chapter 1
## The Community: Elliston

Elliston, originally known as Bird Island Cove,[1] is a community situated far up the Bonavista Peninsula on the north side of Trinity Bay, approximately two hundred miles by road northeast of St. John's. It is a wild place in the sense that it has no proper harbour, being quite as open to the Atlantic as Cape Bonavista itself. The best shelter it has to offer is found in the inlet on the north side of the settlement. Access to the sea is difficult except in two or three places. Yet the fishing was good enough to compensate for the lack of a proper harbour and the dangerous coast. In fact, an agent in the fish trade commented in June, 1813, that "Bonavista and the Bird Islands are allowed to be the best places on the whole coast for fish." It seems only natural, then, that when fishermen could find no more room in the Bonavista area to set up as independent planters they moved further along to this section, probably sometime during the first decade of the nineteenth century.

Between Elliston and Bonavista, five miles to the northwest, stretches a range of hills known as "The Ridge". By the end of the nineteenth century a rough horse-and-cart road crossed this barrier. Before that, travellers had only a footpath. J.V. Nugent in the "First Report upon the Inspection of Schools in Newfoundland," February, 1845, commented: "The road from this place to Catalina has been opened but that to Bonavista has not yet been begun. . . ." Elliston spreads out quite a distance below "The Ridge" and follows the crooks of the coastline. There are no extremely high hills in the community; the land on the whole has a very moderate slope.

The houses in the community are not all situated along one main road. Instead, they are in little clusters, and there are "drungs" [lanes] and roads shooting off in all directions from the main artery. Although it was primarily a fishing community, in some cases the homes are at quite a distance from the sea. Each house has a small plot of land surrounding it, and this area is fenced. In the past, most people had a small vegetable garden and a few had flowers near the house. The meadow land and the main vegetable garden a family possessed might be located one or two miles away from the house.

Elliston has always had several distinct communities; these are mentioned individually in some of the early census returns. Named in order from the section nearest Bonavista these are: North Side, Northern [Noder] Cove, Elliston Centre [The Cove] including Elliston Point [Porter's Point], Sandy Cove, The Neck, Maberly [Muddy Brook], and for a limited period before 1900, Northern [Noder] Bight.

It is only from Church records, business firms' correspondence, and *House of Assembly Journals* that we can obtain any documentary information about early residents in the community. Church records seem to indicate that some moved in from Bonavista during the first decade of the nineteenth century, but there is nothing to tell us how many of these were Newfoundland- born, or how many were recent immigrants. The majority of people living in Elliston today, when asked where their ancestors came from, reply vaguely, "England, somewhere." Others state definitely that this family came from Dorset, this from Devon, and that one from Cornwall. Others are from Ireland. It is probably a safe guess that the majority of the early planters were of West Country stock, and the "youngsters" (bound servants) who came out and stayed were chiefly from the West Country and Ireland.[2]

The area is mentioned in records as early as 1774. At that time "Bonavista merchants, justices of the peace, and others, sent a petition to the governor, Lord Shuldham complaining 'that a number of "masterless" Irishmen (runaway servants) had gone to live in a secluded cove called Bird Island and were there building fishing rooms.'"[3]

My oldest informant, Edwin Baker, said, "When John Chaulk, the first of the settlers, came to Noder Cove, he found two Irishmen, Peter Hackett and Michael Meaney, already fishing from that spot. They made things rather difficult for him so he moved further along the coast to Maberly [Muddy Brook]." Here he found conditions somewhat similar to those in Noder Cove, there being a sizable brook flowing into the sea at this point. It was not, however, as sheltered as Noder Cove. Why he did not choose to settle in Elliston Centre [The Cove] where another large brook flowed into the sea is a mystery. Perhaps he wished to put as much territory between himself and the Irish as possible. The latter moved away with the influx of permanent settlers who followed Chaulk's lead. No one knew or cared where they went.

Church records show that John Chaulk married Mary Flinn in Bonavista on October 11, 1782,[4] and that he died in Bird Island Cove in 1838, aged 85 years. [5]. Those of his descendants who remained in Maberly located in the areas close to the sea and had all the land in the heart of Maberly as well as the best fishing premises (if best there were).

Local tradition does not record what settlers came to Elliston immediately after John Chaulk. Several who were well-established planters by 1813 bore names that are still found in the community.

Those early settlers could not survive unless they could sell their fish and buy the provisions that they could not produce themselves. The important role of the merchant supplier is evident from the records of that period. Not only did he supply needed fishing equipment and provisions, but he was also the settlers' only contact with the Mother Country. Through his offices the planters obtained their "youngsters." Letters and specially ordered household goods, for example, a grandfather clock, came on the company's vessels. Even a small item like a watch needing repairs went through the agent to the appropriate firm back home and returned the same way.

As early as 1813 many Elliston planters dealt chiefly with Slade and Company, a West Country firm from Poole in Dorset. By the time Elliston was settled, this company was well-established in Trinity, thirty miles away. By 1818, a branch of the Slade business had opened in Catalina, ten miles away, and Elliston accounts were transferred to Catalina. The planters now dealt with Catalina, but Trinity still kept control.

Slade and Company continued to supply dealers in Elliston until the middle of the nineteenth century. Some time during that period they must have maintained a store in Elliston, but perhaps only during the summer months. At any rate, a store belonging to Slade and Company was being used as a classroom when the Inspector of Protestant Schools visited the community in 1858.[6]

Names of early planters in Elliston crop up again and again in the

3

Slade records. These names are still found in the community. In a letter written on November 18, 1814, Kelson, the manager at Trinity, lists the number of "youngsters" wanted for the next spring. Included are "one for James Porter of the Bird Islands; two for Thomas Clouter, Bird Islands."[7]

In letters covering the period 1813–1820, Kelson mentions names of other Bird Island residents: Hill, Crew, Brown, Tucker, Burt, Cole, Chard, Trass,[Trask], Felden [Fielding]. Most of these surnames would be considered "Elliston" names even today. George Crew, a native of Dorsetshire, was living in Elliston in 1814, for it was in his home that Ellis, the first Methodist missionary to visit Bird Island Cove, held a religious service.

A "Dealers' List" in the Slade File shows that in 1825 over two hundred males were living in Bird Island Cove. The list names the planters and their "youngsters" and "sharemen" (men paid a share of the voyage), but does not name wives or children. The list, the agent says, does not include all those who dealt with him, only the main ones. From other correspondence in the Slade File, it appears that not all the Elliston planters dealt with the Slade Company, though the greater number did. Excerpts from correspondence between the Trinity and Catalina agents indicate affairs were not always amicable between the Elliston dealers and Slades, but we are not given any details.

Elliston's first permanent settlers appear to have been members of the Church of England. Methodism was first preached in the community in 1814, yet it gained few converts until the mid-1820s. Reverend Lench had this to say in his book *The Story of Methodism in Bonavista:*

> Reverend Ninian Barr reported three members in 1822: George Crew, Elizabeth Crew, and George Brown. These were the "faithful few." Under the ministry of Reverend James Hickson came showers of blessing and in 1825 there were three classes of 71 members.[8]

One can only speculate on the reason why only three people converted to Methodism between 1814 and 1822, while in the three-year interval 1822–1825, the number increased to seventy-one. Perhaps it was due to the personality of Reverend Hickson, but I feel that certain events around that time also played a part. In Philip Tocque's book, *Wandering Thoughts*, written in Elliston during the 1840s, there is a description of a "thunder growl" heard in the Bird Island Cove area some fifteen years before he wrote.

The sound is described as resembling distant thunder. It has also been compared to the growl of a bear, the bellowing of a cow and so on, conveying a deep sepulchural tone. What is most strange and unaccountable is that it appeared alongside of everybody although at the time some were at a distance from each other of from one to five miles.[9]

People were terrified. It is not unlikely that many sought comfort in the evangelism of the early Methodists. Anyway, by the 1880s only a handful of residents belonged to the established Church.

Roman Catholicism practically died out in Elliston when the practice of getting "youngsters" from the Mother Country and Ireland ceased. Except for one man, all the Irish who stayed had turned to Protestantism by the 1900s. The Salvation Army gained some converts by the late 1890s; but though non-Salvationist families helped the Army materially by donations of food and fuel to the "officer," only a few became "soldiers," i.e., adherents of the Army. Still, the Army "meetings" were well attended during the early days of the century. This worshipping in each other's churches was common in Elliston during the early 1900s and later. Methodists, especially the young people, would attend the Anglican church service in the afternoon, and Anglicans would go to the United Church in the evening unless there was an evening service in the Anglican Church. Then both groups attended their respective churches and perhaps went along to the Army later in the night.

My United Church informants in Maberly spoke in the warmest terms of the Church of England minister in the early 1900s, Canon Bayly. They told me they tried to attend all of his Tuesday night services in the Maberly school-chapel. Noah Chaulk said, "We were full of joy to see him." I was brought up in the Anglican tradition, but attended the United Church high school. I was never aware of any animosity between the faiths, though doubtless there were certain people who held very biased views and were intolerant of anything that differed from what they believed.

Certainly there were some sayings that indicate that all was not harmonious. In Elliston I have heard the flat-bottomed tin teakettle referred to as a "flat-assed Methodist," probably referring to the fact that Methodists sat during praying instead of kneeling as Anglicans did. A person who couldn't dance was a "flat-footed Methodist." And I have heard bread having few raisins in it called "Methodist bread."

5

Elliston, then, for the period 1900-1950 was predominantly a Methodist community, or after 1925, a United Church community. In Elliston, United Church was simply a new name for the Methodists. There were no Presbyterians, Congregationalists, etc., to join with them, as was the case in other parts of Canada.

Doubtless during the first decade of settlement before 1820 the residents of Elliston were not overly-concerned with formal schooling. They were planters, who, with grown-up sons and daughters and/or "youngsters," formed a working group involved in making a living and establishing themselves in a new area. By the 1820s, however, the community was established, and if the older people had had any schooling it is natural to assume that they would want the same for their own children and grandchildren. But getting a school set up was no easy task.

The first schooling available outside the home was provided by a missionary of the Society for the Propagation of the Gospel (Anglican) and its successor the Newfoundland School Society during the mid-1820s. The establishment of this "branch" school before the change of denomination, according to the first school inspector for the area, J.V. Nugent (November, 1845), caused Elliston to be overlooked when the government began distributing funds for education, in spite of the fact that a petition had been presented on July 28, 1838. A second petition was presented in 1843 and another in 1850; these, too, were ignored. Finally, in 1854 a school was established in the community, and the teacher was paid from government funds.

For most of the period 1854–1874, one man, William Minty, taught in Elliston. He was a signer of the first petition for instruction in 1838. According to local tradition a man named Mark Chard also taught in Elliston. Both Minty and Chard must have received their education before coming to Newfoundland for both came out as "youngsters" apprenticed to Bird Island Cove planters. Slade's "Dealers' List, 1825" indicates that both men were servants at that time. Chiefly because of their education, which quite likely was superior to that of their employers, Minty and Chard became prominent members of the community when their apprenticeship had been served.

The brief accounts of school inspectors who bothered to visit Bird Island Cove in the 1850s and 60s are usually uncomplimentary. One of them expressed his annoyance with the teacher who refused to call his pupils together for inspection on the day in July the inspector chose to visit the place. The inspector failed to realize a very important fact of outport living: in mid-July all the pupils would be involved in the fishery itself, or replacing the mothers at home so the latter could help with the fish. Besides, the teacher himself had to work at the fishery during the summer in order to get a living. His meagre £25 was £5 less than that received by the Newman's Cove teacher who served a much smaller community. Apparently the difference in salary arose because Bird Island Cove was in Trinity District under the Anglican board where government funds were spread more thinly than in Bonavista District.

In the early 1880s the Elliston school finally came under the Methodist Board for Bonavista and Peter Moores came to teach in the community. Shortly thereafter, "Church" people built a school in Maberly where Miss Annie Tilly went to teach. From that time on there were women, as well as men, teaching in the several Elliston schools — Maberly, Neck, Elliston Centre, and North Side.

It would seem that many children of the better-off families got much of their early schooling at home, even though there was a school in the community. Ernest Tilly, born April 15, 1873, mentioned in an article in *The Newfoundland Quarterly*[10] in 1958 that he was ten years old when he went to school to Peter Moores. He ran away the first day, and his father let him continue his reading under his Aunt Nell's tutelage. She brought him along to long division in arithmetic and he went to Thomas Tilly for "higher mathematics." Pupils of "The Missus" in Maberly also went to Thomas Tilly for mathematics. Although Aunt Annie's field was not mathematics, she was an excellent reader, and her old pupils still recall how well she could explain a passage of prose.

Over the years the residents of Elliston had sent numerous petitions to the government for help in establishing a school. They sent as many, if not more, on another important matter: roads. Obviously they felt that connections with the larger trading centres of Bonavista and Catalina were absolutely vital to them. Most of their trading had to be done through these communities because it was too difficult to bring goods in or ship them out from such an unprotected spot as Elliston. In 1844 Inspector Nugent reported there was a rough road to Catalina and a start made on the Bonavista one. By the early 1900s rough horse-and-cart roads had been built in the community itself and between Elliston and Bonavista and Catalina. Again, it should be stressed that the only reason for the existence of a community in such a wild section of coast was its nearness to rich fishing grounds. Through the years Elliston's fortunes have been governed by the success or failure of the inshore cod fishery.

With such nearly total dependence on the fishery, a bad year at this end of the Bonavista Peninsula meant hardship for all. "Poor fisheries and an occasional semi-potato famine brought the people into dire straits," wrote Reverend Charles Lench in 1918.[11]

As with other fishing communities in Newfoundland, the initial phase of settlement by planters with their servants was over some time in the 1830s. During this period there was little need for women to work at the fish: splitting, salting, drying, though some women servants probably did. When the inshore fishery became a family affair, that is, when the planter's servants and sharemen struck out for themselves, a woman who knew how to work at the fish became a real necessity to a successful fisherman.

From 1830 to 1950, the chores a woman had in connection with the fishery depended on the size and kind of crew her husband was in.

Fishing crews varied considerably in size depending on whether they used hand lines and trawls or trapped fish. One man might go hand-lining alone; they called it fishing "cross-handed." Usually three men would be considered enough for a hand-lining crew but a trap crew often had five or six members.

Many crews were essentially family groups, with the father as skipper and his grown sons as crew. On the death of the parent, the eldest son usually became skipper, and, provided there were not too many brothers and they could get along together, they would continue to fish as a unit. If, for any reason another crew was formed, say one of the brothers and his grown sons, the new crew often would continue to share the same fishing premises but would have separate fish-storing facilities. Some crews might be made up of a couple of brothers, plus one or two sharemen, who could be related, perhaps by marriage, but there might be no family connection. Sharemen usually stayed with the same crew for years. When brothers or a father and his sons fished in partnership, the woman of the family was expected to help with the fish work. I do not believe wives of sharemen normally worked at the fish. I cannot say for certain just what the practice was, for the sharemen I knew were unmarried men.

The inshore cod fishery was the main work but the only thing certain about it was the uncertainty. Fish might be scarce during some seasons, and even in those years when they were plentiful the fisherman did not receive a high price for his catch. Families had to have other ways to help make ends meet and here again the women were extensively involved.

Although Elliston has never been a farming community, since the

8

earliest days subsistence farming had been practiced. Most families grew enough vegetables to last all year long. Since all but the poorest families kept animals: cows, goats, and sheep, for milk, meat, and wool, and dogs or horses for hauling, the families had to make enough hay for fodder during the winter. Wild and home-grown fruits added variety to the community's tables. Bakeapples, blueberries, and partridge berries were picked and preserved for the winter but it was not until the mid-twentieth century when blueberries, and partridge berries fetched $0.50 — $0.80 a gallon that berry picking provided a valuable supplement to families' incomes. Many families made enough on berries some years to buy their food supplies for the winter.

In Elliston there has never been any local employment except fishing and jobs related to it. In the fishing industry the fisherman is the supplier of the product. Once he delivers the fish to the merchant or plant he has nothing further to do with it. When the fish was shipped, that is, sold, to the local merchant, C. Tilley, Ltd., jobs were provided for a few men who looked after it until it was exported. When fish was packed in wooden casks, local coopers were kept busy for a time making the containers. The fisherman though, unless he did well at the fishery, had to go elsewhere to make a decent living.

Before 1900, and during the first decade or so of the twentieth century, many men went "to the ice" each spring. Until the branch railway was extended to Bonavista, sealers from Elliston had to walk to Port Blandford in Bonavista Bay to take the passenger boat to St. John's, where most of the crews were "signed on."

Sealing was in its heyday around 1914, but there were two great sealing disasters that spring: the "*Newfoundland* Disaster" on the Front and the *Southern Cross* in the Gulf. Eight men from Elliston died on the ice in the "*Newfoundland* Disaster," and two came back badly frostbitten. Fewer men went sealing after that, but this might be partly because some went off to fight in the First World War and others became lumberjacks each winter when the lumber camps opened up to supply the paper mills at Grand Falls (1909) and Corner Brook (1923). For years the majority of men followed the pattern of summer fishing and winter lumbering. Because this woods' work kept the man of the house away from home for perhaps five or six months at a time, a greater burden of responsibility was placed on women during the twentienth century than before that time. Life was never easy. It is not surprising that there has been a constant exodus of the younger people from Elliston. Even in the late 19th

9

century many had left the community — though not always to stay away. And those who went to work away from the community were few compared to the outflow of the '20s. The women who left in this early period usually went "into service" with a family in a nearby community, perhaps Bonavista or Catalina. Some went farther, however. My Grandmother Chaulk went to King's Cove, Bonavista Bay where she was the "inside maid" for the Anglican clergyman's family. As a child I was told how she walked the entire distance. The path went through the woods, wound over "windfalls" (fallen trees), and at times was perilously near the edge of the cliffs. I do not know whether she made the journey alone or not. I have one momento of that period of her life — a letter dated February, 1879, written to her by her father, Samuel Porter.

The coming of the branch railway to Bonavista made movement easier and gave people a better chance to get away. My Mother and a friend of hers from the North Side, having finished school in Elliston, attended Normal School in St. John's during the summer of 1917. Mother's teaching career was confined entirely to Maberly but several other women of her generation went all over the Island to take up teaching posts. Others went to St. John's "in service."

Emigration to the United States was the path that many young people chose especially during the 1920s. I mentioned that nearly every family in the community had relatives in the States. My Father's older brother Albert had gone before the 1914 war. Consequently instead of serving with the Newfoundland Regiment he went overseas with the Canadian Forces. His other brother and his two sisters went during the 20s. This was the pattern of emigration followed by most families in the community.

Although many young men went off to war during 1914–1918, the First World War did not disrupt the work patterns or way of life of the community. However, during the Second World War, 1939–1945, not only did many of the younger men go off to war, but also older men gave up fishing to fill jobs on the various American bases in different parts of the Island, particularly Gander. Many of these men stayed with "base work" after the war.

Certainly one can say that since the beginning of the 20th century young people of both sexes have been leaving Elliston in great numbers. This has been accelerated since the '50s and the better opportunities for higher education provided by the University in St. John's and the vocational schools in different parts of the island. Confederation and the lure of jobs on the Mainland took many during the '50s and '60s. Others left to live and work in Labrador.

Only a handful of those who remain in the community are permanently employed: a half dozen government employees, e.g., teachers and post office personnel; and a small group of sales clerks and managers of branch stores. There are three or four small local shops and a few small fishing crews. Some families get by on seasonal work which the father manages to find inside or outside the community. The majority of the residents are elderly and live on government pensions, and a number are unemployed.

# Chapter 2
## Making a Living:
## "The Woman was More Than 50%"

In Elliston, in the period prior to 1950, the women were full participants with their menfolk in wresting a living from the sea and land, and were directly involved with all the economic, as well as social activities in the community. The role of the fisherman's wife was completely intertwined with that of her husband. As one man, Josiah Hobbs, put it:

> The woman was more than fifty per cent. In some cases there was more push in the woman than there was . . . if there was fish, to get fish, than there was in the man. The woman was more for fishin' even though she stopped on the land. She was the driving force. And they all took . . . I should say, a woman, in a fisherman's work, was half of the procedure. . . .

The consensus among my older informants was that if a man married a lazy woman, "he was finished, he'd get nowhere." Josiah's wife Maud even went so far as to state: "The woman was the mainstay of the family." Other elderly male informants admitted: "Couldn't have been done without the women." In some cases, as Noah Chaulk said, "Women worked just as hard or harder than the men. All is in it they didn't break as much rest as the men," i.e. the women could sleep a bit longer in the morning. But the women worked after the men were through. Men could sleep during the day if occasion arose, for example, if during the trapping season they had a "water haul," i.e., no fish at all in the cod trap.

12

It is true that women did not rise as early as men, for men who were hand-lining might get up at two or three a.m. But some women began their household chores very early in the morning, at dawn if it was a good trapping season and if they expected to be working at the fish all day. And dawn comes very early at that time of the year. Besides, every night before retiring, the women laid the table for the menfolk to have a light breakfast before they left the house. Also, they often laid out the men's workclothes in orderly fashion for their convenience.

No woman in Elliston went catching cod, but this was the only part of the operation in which she was not involved. On shore she might do any job, for in the preparation of fish for market, or home use, "men's work" and "women's work" might be interchangeable. The work a woman did depended on the size of the fishing crew and the men's attitude. With a large crew, the many tasks could be spread around, and she might have one specialized job; but with a small crew, she might be required to do more of the jobs, even those generally thought of as being "mens' work" because they required considerable strength or a particular skill.

Any of the operations performed in "putting away" a boatload of fish might be done by a woman: bringing approximately 200 pounds of fish at a time in a "tub bar" (a half-barrel carried by two people using two poles as handles) from the "stagehead", the wharf onto which the fish were thrown from the boat, to the "splitting tee", a temporary hut covered with tar paper and thatched with boughs; putting the fish, weighing five to ten pounds each on the "splitting table", where the cutting-open process began; "cutting throats", slitting the fish's throat and belly nearly to the tail; "heading", breaking off the head and taking out the stomach, etc.; "splitting", taking out the "soundbone", i.e., the backbone; washing, prior to salting; "laying away", putting fish down face up, one by one, in rows in barrels or rectangular piles; "salting", throwing on sufficient coarse salt to cure the fish; — any of these operations performed in "putting away" a boatload of fish might be done by a woman. However, "heading", which required brute strength, was generally done by a man; and splitting was usually done by the skipper himself. Splitters took great pride in the speed and precision with which they could do their work.

In summer, fishermen's wives were expected to combine homemaking with long hours of work outside the home, either at the fishery or at the gardens. All the men who fished were in the inshore fishery and either went "fishing," that is used hook and line and/or trawls, or operated cod traps, i.e., fixed nets. The trapmen too went "fishing" early in the season, early June, or after the trapping season which only lasted from late June to late July, was past. Before 1900, all the fishermen worked with hand lines or trawls, or cod seines; the routine at that time differed somewhat from the one followed after they began using traps in the first decade of the twentieth century.

A woman's workday in summer was governed largely by whether her husband was handlining or trapping. If her husband were a handliner, the crew would likely be a small one, and each member might be required to attend to several jobs in the curing operation but there would, at the most, be only one boatload a day to put away, and she would not have to spend all day working at the fish. Hence, the wife of a handliner could do her housework at a more leisurely pace than the wife of a trapman when lots of fish were being caught.

It usually happened that women had more to do with the final curing processes than did the men. "Making the fish," i.e., looking after the drying on "flakes", open elevated wooden platforms built of round sticks covered with boughs, was entirely the women's responsibility if the men were still catching fish when the drying process began. In the early days, most "hook and line" fish were cured "in pickle" which meant that they had to be "washed out" and dried on the flake after being in salt for only a short period, perhaps two weeks. "In the old days," said Noah Chaulk "they were often fishing and making it at the same time."

One woman whose husband fished "cross-handed" did all the work with the final curing of the fish herself. Her husband had an outfit made so that she could "carry out" his fish (move the washed salted fish from the stage to the flake for drying). It was a frame, probably a yoke across her shoulders, and two containers.

The routine followed by a trapman's wife was very different from that of the handliner's wife, when fish were plentiful. As a member of a large trapping crew, she would have a specialized job to attend to, but she would have to handle thousands of fish in a single boatload and there might be five boatloads to put away in a single day.

The latter's family expected "mug-ups" or "lunches" before beginning work on each boatload of fish. A hearty breakfast had to be ready for them when they arrived in the kitchen at 7:30–8:00 a.m. They would have already moved the first load of fish from the boat to the splitting tee. Breakfast over, all would head for the stage, the wife or mother slightly behind as she would have to tidy her kitchen before leaving it.

After each boatload had been put away, the men of the crew headed for the trap again, while the women hurried to the kitchen to prepare a quick meal and get some household chores done. These mug-ups were often just bread and butter with tea, but the fourth meal of the day, served around noon, was a substantial one, consisting usually of fish — either fried, boiled, stewed, or baked — and potatoes. Trapmen's wives had to serve seven meals a day, on days when there were five or six boatloads of fish to put away.

Fuel that burned easily was needed "to boil the kettle" quickly. Most women liked to use "blassy boughs," dry, blasted, red branches of fir trees, for a quick, hot, fire. In the early 1900s women were expected "to keep the stove going" during the summer, and they brought bundles or "loads" of boughs tied up with rope on their backs from areas several miles away from the community. In the 1930s and 40s, although "blassy" boughs were still a favourite summer fuel, women rarely collected them. In those years, men and boys would "go for a load of boughs" when they got a "slack moment." But women and girls cut them into suitable pieces and kept the wood-box filled.

It was indeed fortunate for trapmen's wives that they had to maintain a hectic pace for a short period of three to four weeks only. No person could have stood the long hours of standing at heavy work in the stage, plus all the many household duties performed without benefit of today's modern conveniences. "Stage work" was a communal activity and was lightened by a yarn, a song, a joke. Laughter helped the work along.

Even though she knew it meant much extra work for her, the fisherman's wife was always pleased to see that the "rodney," the small rowboat, had been left behind with the "bagged fish"[1] and the motor boat was steaming towards the land — water touching her "gunnels" (gunwales) she carried such a whopping load. Plenty of fish meant "good living" during the year, provided the price of the finished product were a good one.

Trapping crews usually put most of their fish in "salt bulk," i.e. dry-salted in big rectangular piles, and worked as a unit — men and women — to "wash out" the salted fish. This was put in "water horse," the washed fish, back up, in rectangular piles, overnight till the water pressed out of it. Men generally moved the washed out fish from the stage to the flake by "handbar" loads. All the men in the crew worked on the flake if they were ashore; but if they were handlining, the flake work was left almost entirely to the woman.

The skipper's wife took charge of the "flake work" if the men were away fishing, and she had to be a good "skipper" herself, as well as a good judge of weather. She had to decide whether they would wash out fish, how much fish they would spread in the morning, and what lots were not to be spread out because usually the fish being cured were at various stages of dryness.

There was a certain pattern to be followed in spreading and "taking up" fish at different stages of cure. Said Aunt Hilda

It was first taken up with a small fish placed over a large one, both back up. Care had to be taken with the big "pickle" fish when taking them up for the first time, especially if it were a Saturday. Sunday might be hot and the big ones might sunburn if left unshielded. Next evening we put four fish together, heads and tails. Then small "faggots", then larger "faggots" (i.e., rectangular piles nicely rounded on the top). When the fish dried hard they were put in a big round pile.

Only one or two of the adults would be allowed to put fish in the pile, for this was a skilled task. Those building it had to lay the fish straight and flat, and had to make sure to put enough fish in the centre to keep the pile even. The rest of the people working on the flake were kept busy bringing "yaffles," i.e., armloads, of fish to those making the pile. Both faggots and "big piles" in the early 1900s and in the 1940s were covered with "rinds," i.e., twelve to fourteen inch wide strips of tree bark, length about four to five feet, to protect from rain and dew. These were held down with heavy rocks. When fish had dried to a certain stage, it was stored in the "fish store" or "fish loft" for a few days, "to work."

On a dry, sunny day in late August, the flakes would be filled with very dry fish and "shipping" would begin. Shipping fish meant to sell it to the local fish merchant at a given rate per quintal, 112 pounds. Until the 1940s, all the fish was carted to the merchant's premises by horse cart. In later years, it was moved in trucks. Now and then during the summer some women, if they needed something special at the local store, would take three or four cured fish and barter them for what they needed.

Most of the flake work was done during August when the main season for catching fish was finished. By the end of September, if the catch was mostly "light salted," work with the fish would be just about over. However, if the fish had been "heavy salted" or in "salt bulk", the crew would be busy curing a large catch during October, or even into Novem-

16

ber. But to be busy with fish so late in the season was rare indeed in Elliston.

My informants spoke highly of the woman's contribution to the fishery in the period before 1950, but they were well aware of the other aspects of her outdoor work:

> Women took a major part in raising vegetables. The garden was the woman's responsibility, weeding and looking after it. The woman played a major role in that, see, you understand, said Josiah Hobbs.

Every fisherman in Elliston had, or could have, sufficient land on which to raise the necessary vegetables for his family's use and grass for his animals. If a family did not grow its own vegetables, it would have to do without, for, unlike today, vegetables were not obtained from the local grocery stores. And people had to keep their own animals: cows, sheep, goats, and horses, if they wished to have meat, milk, wool and hauling power. Families had pieces of land of varying shapes and sizes in different parts of the community. Some of these might be entirely in grass and within the main "grass garden", there might be plots about 18' by 20' for carrots or turnips, and a 200' by 500' plot for potatoes.

Stable manure was used as fertilizer on both grass ground and vegetable patches, but the latter was also covered with "kelp," i.e., seaweed, in late fall. Men and boys, working with horse and plough, or with sharp pointed shovels, ploughed or dug this fertilizer into the potato ground each spring. Women and girls had to prepare the ground for all other vegetables.

Women's first work in the garden for the year began in the meadow in early spring. Women and children were responsible for "picking the ground," i.e., collecting all the debris that had accumulated on the grass land over the winter.

Women might help with the "potato cutting," cutting a whole potato into several pieces, each with an eye for seed but if the men had no other pressing work to attend to, they often did this job in one of the outbuildings. Potatoes were sown by both men and women. The seeds were set in raised "beds" separated by deep trenches. Each sower wore a "pratie" (potato) bag, a sort of pouch, tied around his middle, containing a supply of seed. Using a square-tipped spade with a wooden "ear" attached just over the blade, either on the right or left side, the sower made a hole by forcing the spade into the soil through pressure on the ear. Pushing it slightly forward, he dropped a seed in the silt, the spade was lifted up, and the soil dropped back into the slit covering the seed. In some families, once the potato seed had been sown, the men had nothing further to do with the garden until the crop was harvested in the fall.

The vegetables were fertilized during the summer with materials from the sea, but always by the women: caplin, in quantity, for potatoes; cods' heads with the "putticks," i.e., stomachs, attached for turnips and cabbages; and "soundbones," i.e., fish's backbones, or caplin for carrot and parsnip. Aunt Hilda told me that after the cods' heads were placed on the cabbage patch and rotted, the skeleton or bony part was taken off, and the soil underneath was shoveled around the cabbage roots. However, when cods' heads were put in a turnip patch, the skeleton was not removed.

In many families, the men did the difficult job of "trenching" potatoes. This was done after the fish fertilizer had been placed on the potato beds by the women. The men dug up the space between the beds and placed the loosened earth on the fish. The trenching covered up the fish fertilizer, thus cutting down on the bad smell and also reducing the number of weeds.

Several of my informants remarked that there were no insects to bother crops in the early years. One man, William Crewe, said that he believed it was because there were lots of birds then to eat up the insects. "It was hard to keep the plants in the ground when the birds were after the insects." They grew "wonderful" cabbages — "big as kettles." But they did not grow the same crops in the same spot year after year. Said Mr. Crewe, "need to change over for good results" (i.e., practice rotation). The older people believed, said Betsy Crewe, that "home-grown" seed was better than "bought" seed. Aunt Hilda echoed this sentiment when she said.

> They thought if they bought cabbage and turnip seed from the store the flies would eat it. They felt their own was much better. Besides a woman was considred lazy if she did not grow her own seeds. Usually she kept back the very best of her turnips and the very best cabbage which she planted in a special spot for them "to go to seed.' Most people grew their own seed.

Weeding the potatoes, sowing, thinning out and weeding all other vegetables, was always the woman's responsibility until the 1940s. Weeding the potatoes, the staple crop, was often a long job and a back-breaking one. It was a job that had to be done correctly, too. There could be no

18

weeds left, no broken-off weeds, and no tumbled beds. A poorly weeded garden was a sign of laziness on the part of the woman in the household. This was probably why most women preferred to do their own weeding; outsiders would not take the same care with the job.

This I remember very vividly, for one summer my mother *employed two* women who were not involved with the fishery to weed her potato garden. They did it so poorly, that pressed as she was for time because of her work with the fish, she weeded it over again herself. She couldn't have her garden looking so messy. Most weeding was done early in the morning before tasks connected with the fishery had begun. Sometimes, it was a job which got done in "dribs and drabs," sandwiched in between other chores on a day when there was little doing with the fish. To keep the mosquitoes away in the days before fly repellents became common, women tucked tansy into a scarf tied around the forehead. Its odour kept the flies off fairly well. Although weeding was hard work, it seems one woman did not think it so. She was heard to remark one summer's day, sometime in the 1930s: "Think I'll go out and weed me garden while I'm havin' a spell" (i.e., rest). Perhaps she believed in the saying, "A change is as good as a rest."

Because the fishermen kept animals, they had to provide winter feed for them. Hay was the staple diet, though the horse, the favourite of the stable, had his diet enriched with oats now and then. However, these were not grown locally, though some did spring up and grow wild. During July, the men cut the grass with long-handled scythes (sives). In smaller areas, they might also use sickles or "rip-hooks" (reaphooks).

"Making grass" was frequently a family affair, with everyone available helping, but it was the woman who did most of the work with it. First the grass was scattered free of the long scythe swards. After the first day of drying, the grass was raked into rolls with wooden rakes. The next evening, it was placed in tiny "pooks," i.e., stacks, all over the garden; next day larger pooks were made, and finally one large pook located in the middle of the cut-over area. Those who were raking up the grass were expected to get every straw; the ground could not be left in an untidy condition. besides, the hay pook had to be as symmetrical as possible. One family's pooks (Thomas Tilly's) were always so well made that they were objects of admiration for everyone in the community.

Wet or damp grass was never stored in the "loft" for "fear of fire." If the men were on shore when it was time to store the hay they always carried it in bundles, often on their backs. If the garden was a long way from

19

the storage area, the hay was moved with horse and cart. Often women would store small amounts themselves, but only if the men were not around.

A great many families kept goats or cows. Those who kept the latter often made butter for their families. One woman, Mrs. Charles Trask, said that during two or three summers they kept two 'milch' cows. One cow she remembered was an exceptionally good milker. "She'd come home and she'd have her udder draggin' on the ground." The milk was rich in cream and she always made butter.

> Two or three pounds of butter at one time. And do it up in little prints. I had a printer with a cow on it. I'd stick it on and when it'd print it on . . . the printer on the butter . . . you'd see the cow on there, her tits stickin' off. 'Twas grand.

Most of her butter she

> put in a butter tub, used to be going then you know. I'd put it down in the butter tub and put a bit of salt on it and keep it there for months and months.

Women who kept goats did not have such a great supply of milk. They "scalded" (heated to boiling point) each day's milk every morning and had just enough to last through the day. Milk was never drunk straight from the animal; this was not considered clean. It had to be strained, i.e., passed through a thin cloth to remove any foreign matter, and then scalded.

Fortunately, the work pattern in summer was not a rigid one; it varied to suit the kind of fishing and the weather. One day might find a woman working in the stage, on the flake, in the garden, at the grass, and of course in the house; another might be more slowly paced, for if it were a rainy or foggy day, work on the flake or at the grass would be eliminated. On such a day she might get a chance to do important jobs in the garden like weeding or thinning out vegetables.

There were many days, though, when a woman seemed to be needed in a dozen places at once. It was just such a day which caused one informant, Betsy Crewe, to say to herself as she moved from one task to another: "Killing ourselves, working like this and when we clews up we won't have a copper to put on our eyes." She had reason to complain that year, for there were lots of fish, but it was "no price," that is, had to be sold very cheaply, leaving them with hardly enough to pay expenses. Another, Orpah Crewe, spoke of working "in the stage, on the flake, in the house, at the gardens, at the grass, no let up, the women worked harder than the men,"

Gardening,for most women meant tending to vegetables or hay-making. Few families "wasted" good ground in flower gardens. There were a few housewives, however, whose families were perhaps a bit better off in terms of land than others in the community, who did have flower gardens. And here along with the sweet rocket, columbine, lilies, daisies, and roses, they grew herbs like tansy, mint and chive which were used in medicine and cooking. Here,too, was found the rhubarb patch and the black currant bushes. The latter were important because every good housewife kept a little black "curn" (currant) jam on hand to ease sore throats.

Although nearly every house in Elliston was "fenced in" and had a front garden as well as a back yard, many of the front gardens held vege-tables like carrot, beet, cabbage, even potato. For a man with a large fam-ily and little land needed every available inch, either to grow vegetables for the family, or grass for the animals.

By late July or early August the hay would be made and there was nothing to be done in the vegetable garden till mid-October. The house-wife, however, still had work connected with the outdoors, for this was the season for gathering bakeapples (*rubus chamaemorus*) which grow wild on marshland. There was no market for bakeapples until recently, but every-one tried to have bakeapple jam for the winter. Non-Newfoundlanders can never understand why natives like this seedy jam so much. Sometimes the soft juicy berries were packed into jars and liberally covered with sug-ar, but usually the berries were jammed, that is, boiled with lots of sugar, and then put in glass jars. These jars had to be as tight as possible other-wise the jam would quickly spoil; housewives did not use paraffin to seal the jars.

Blueberries (*vaccinium angustifolium*) were the first wild berries gath-ered for sale, but their season was short, and they were never overly abun-dant. In the early years there was no sale for blueberries at all, so they were picked for home use only, for jam and wine, but the jam did not keep well. It was not till comparatively recently that women put them in Mason jars and steamed them. So blueberries for home use were used chiefly for making wine. Most women liked to get the berries for wine just

21

after the first frost, as they were best for wine making then. Everyone liked to have some blueberry wine for Christmas, unless they were very strict teetotalers. Since the thirties, the sale of blueberries has provided a valuable supplement to the family economy. Women picking blueberries for sale, went to the berry grounds or "barrens" carrying perhaps two water buckets and a hoop (yoke) as for water. Each one also had a smaller container, a quart can, saucepan, perhaps even a gallon can. As this "emper" or "emptier" was filled, its contents were transferred to the buckets till these were filled to the brim, that is if the berries were plentiful. Women usually went in groups of two or three for blueberries, sometimes taking along smaller children who picked berries as well. Rarely did family groups go blueberry picking.

The men frequently went on their own, or they might take the older boys in the family. Often they went farther away from the community and travelled over more difficult terrain, where the women with their buckets and hoops, would find it difficult to go. Men usually carried their blueberries in a "berry box" holding about six or seven gallons. This was a rectangular wooden box, fitted with a hinged cover and having two rope loops about one-third the way down, through which the man thrust his arms. It was carried very much like a knapsack would be. Often there was an additional loop at the other side, or at the back of the box, through which he thrust a stick or pole which lodged on his shoulder and thus made the load easier to carry.

Partridge berries (*vaccinium vitis-idaea*), usually abundant, were the easiest of all to preserve, and would keep indefinitely. Women preserved gallons of these and put them away in glass jars ready for eating at any time. Some berries they "jammed down," that is, boiled them up with a little sugar. Before these berries could be used, they had to be cooked again with extra sugar. This boiled-down mixture was also stored in glass jars. A third method was simply to put ten or twelve gallons of berries in a small wooden barrel or keg and add a little water. The housewife could take out berries and cook them as needed. Water and freezing did not alter the taste of the partridge berries very much.

Partridge berries sold for a higher price than blueberries. Some families picked many barrels of them during a season. (One barrel — twenty gallons.) One person might pick over twenty gallons per day at the start of the season. Most people, even children, could easily manage ten or twelve gallons per day. When they sold for only ten cents a gallon it was hard work for very little return, but in the forties when they might range in price from 50–80 cents a gallon, it was a godsend when they were abundant, especially after a poor fishing season.

Family groups often went partridge berry picking together. People always carried lunches to the berry grounds and "boiled-up" around midday. The container or emper in which partridge berries were gathered was often bigger than that used for blueberries. The men often used "berry pickers" (scoops with wire teeth) to gather them if they struck a good patch.

The berries were always cleaned on the barrens. People did this by slowly pouring the berries from a height into a tablecloth or a bucket so that the wind would blow away the twigs and leaves. All rotten and unripe berries were spotted at this time and removed. Sometimes when the berries were picked on a very wet day, the leaves stuck to them and did not blow away. Such berries would have to be cleaned again at home by the mother. Since partridge berries were firmer than blueberries, at least early in the season, the men and women carried them home in 100 pound flour bags or bigger burlap sacks. Later in the fall when the berries became juicy and also scarcer, they were carried home in buckets and boxes, in the same manner as blueberries and for the same reasons.

Berries were "shipped" or sold to the local merchant or merchants, who were agents for St. John's-based firms. No money changed hands at least until the 1950s. Those who sold berries were given a "berry note" indicating the amount of berries shipped and the price per gallon. The value of the note had to be "taken up" in goods in the store where the berries were shipped. A family of five or six good berry pickers could, in a good season, provide the family with some necessary food items purchased from the store — flour, margarine, sugar, molasses, beef, pork, etc. — and get winter clothing as well. Berrying would be carried on sometimes till November, but the majority of people, certainly the women, would have stopped by mid-October.

After the berrying season was over, the basic crop, potatoes, was harvested. This work involved the whole family, but if the father were away in the lumberwoods, the mother and children got the vegetables in the best they could. If the men were at home, it was usually they who did the digging. Children or women hauled stalks, and my Aunt Hilda told me that when she hauled stalks as a child she had to be very sure to leave every potato in the bed; the diggers did not want the potatoes scattered around the bed. Women usually "picked up" that is, gathered the potatoes from the ground after they had dried off a bit and put them in "brin" (burlap) bags. As they gathered the dried-off potatoes, they graded them, leaving the very small ones in piles on the ground. These were gathered later and stored separately, as they were fed to the pig or the chickens during the winter. Men usually carried the potatoes from the garden to the root cellar, but if they were absent, women did this in smaller loads. All other vegetables were lifted by the women. Again, men might carry them to the cellar as this was heavy work.

Most vegetables were stored in root cellars and the only one that needed special attention was cabbage. Usually the best heads were "pickled," that is, salted in a barrel in a manner similar to the way fish were treated. A layer of cabbage was laid down and then a layer of coarse salt. Sometimes a little beef pickle was added to give a special flavour. Kept tightly covered, "salted cabbage" could last a long time, but the housewife had to remember to soak it thoroughly overnight before cooking it. Otherwise, it would be "like the brine," i.e., too salty to eat.

Usually, when the husband "settled up" in the fall, that is, settled his debts to the merchant and received any cash coming to him after the purchase of winter supplies, he gave this money to his wife. Likewise, any money earned "away" was given to the wife to look after when the man returned home. The woman handled the cash and managed the day to day running of the household.

After the potatoes and other vegetables had been harvested in the fall, women normally had no further outside work to attend to. Chores, like taking care of the stock, getting vegetables from the cellar, bringing in the firewood, bringing the daily supply of water, were done by women in the summer but by the men and boys in the winter. Perhaps this change-over in winter resulted from the fact that winter was a slow season for the men. If they were at home, they were mainly responsible for getting the year's supply of firewood from the "country," whereas the women were extremely busy indoors with carding, spinning, knitting, sewing, mat hooking, etc. About the only job a man did indoors was the "knitting of twine" (netting to replace worn-out sections in the cod trap before it was placed in the water for another fishing season) during the late winter or early spring. Women and children helped by filling the shuttlelike needles with the twine.

If, however, her husband were "away working" during the winter months, a woman and her children would have to look after the necessary outdoor chores. But if it was a "young family," a neighbour who did not have a job away from home might be asked by the man of the house to look after some of the outside jobs, especially during stormy winter weather.

Women did not ordinarily go to the woods for firewood in wintertime. This was men's work but I was told, by her sister of one exceptional woman who did it:

> I believe she was the only one in here used to do it. She used to go in the woods, see maid, you see her, she was like a man, a boy. She used to take the slide and the dogs and her whip and go in, you'd see her goin' in and comin' out with her slide. George was only two years old, young see, so she used to say she was his (father's) boy. George was always sick see. And I was the oldest and I used to be sick. I wasn't able to do nothing hardly, cause I was sick. But poor Sare Ann was a proper boy. They used to call her Uncle Tom's boy. And she used to go in the woods with her slide and dog every mornin' in the week, goin' it, haulin' out the wood.

The wood, of course, had been cut by her father earlier. This unusual woman did other jobs generally considered men's work. For example when seals were killed on the ice near the community, she went off on the ice with her father and towed, i.e. dragged, back two seals at a time to the shore.

In most households, carding and spinning wool and knitting it into garments, "fancy work," sewing (making clothing and "joining quilts"), and hooking mats (rag rugs), were considered women's late fall and winter occupations. But the preliminaries to knitting spanned the seasons. Sheep were sheared in the late spring, usually in May, and someone would be sure to note that the weather turned cold for a few days after the majority of sheep had been shorn. In some families, the mother and daughters did the shearing; in others, husband and wife co-operated on this job. Some people tied the sheep's legs; others simply held them down. Shearing was done with ordinary household scissors. It was a job that most women loathed because sheep invariably had "ticks" which sometimes bit the shearers.

After the shearing, the wool was washed. One woman told me that she always put hers in brin bags and placed them in running water in the brook. The bags were weighted down so that they would not float away. Then the "fleece" was rinsed and often hung on the fence to dry. The wool was usually stored during the summer. Sometimes if a woman had a little "slack" time during the summer, she might "pick some wool." But this job of removing twigs and any other foreign matter from the wool, was usually the children's job later in the fall. After "picking," the wool was ready for carding.

Carding[2] was generally a late fall occupation. The carder worked with two cards. These were two rectangular thin pieces of board, perhaps 8″ by 4″; each had a short wooden handle attached to the back and the front of each was filled with fine wire teeth, something like a scrubbing brush. A small portion of matted wool was placed on the toothed face of the cards, and the other was drawn across it two or three times, catching the fibres, in its teeth. The carder pulled the cards backwards and forwards through the wool until she got a nice smooth rectangular roll, slightly rounded in the centre. This was then placed in a pile for spinning at a later time. Jane Pearce was careful to make this point.

> You take them off 'roundy'. Some'd take 'um off flat, but they're not so good. Take them off on the back of your card and do that with your hand see (a deft smoothing motion) and you'd spin that out as good again.

Not every woman in the community could spin, and there was a great deal of difference in the quality of yarn produced by different spinners. Some were "expert with that wheel," said Aubrey Pearce. Aunt Hilda said her mother varied the size of the wool she spun so that she had the type she needed for different times. She made big yarn for the heavy work mitts, small yarn for the men's stockings, and for the girls' stockings she spun it as fine as the three ply wool which can be bought nowadays in the stores. Others, who were poor spinners, turned out yarn very uneven in texture; but the majority seemed to have turned out a suitable product to serve their family's needs.

It was strange indeed to find a woman who could neither spin nor knit, but Jane Pearce, an excellent spinner and knitter herself did not learn at home. Apparently her mother could neither spin nor knit. She did not explain why her mother lacked these very necessary skills of a "good" housewife. Perhaps her mother was orphaned when quite young and had no one at home to teach her. But, if so, she lacked the talent and desire to learn that her daughter possessed, for the latter learned from the neighbours. Here is how she described her way of learning:

26

I'll tell 'e how I got that now, maid. In the evenings when I'd go around — I was never no good to learn - I mean the education (school book) but I'd go around anyone's house and see 'um then cardin' wool. I was only small and I'd see what they'd do. And when I'd see 'um cardin' I'd say: "Why can't I do that?" And I'd take up the cards when they'd put 'um down. I'd take 'um up and try 'um and I learnt cardin. And I'd see 'um with the spinnin' wheel. I used to always go to Aunt Polly's and Polly'd go out in the stable somewhere and I used to say: "I wonder can I run her wheel?" And I'd give it a try. So nice, and I said "I can spin." . . . I was all there for that. Go in anyone's house and see them sewing on the machine. I could knit sweaters, and stockin's and mitts, gloves, do anything. My mother never showed me cause Mother never knowed how to knit. I learned meself now, like that. I could do anything.

Apparently this woman never thought to ask any woman to teach her how to do any of these things. She, like most of her generation, was probably too shy and hesitant to make such a request. But she watched every move they made in spinning, carding, knitting,sewing etc., and then imitated them in her best fashion when there was no one around to criticise her first attempts. For instance, she did not touch the spinning wheel until the woman using it had left the room on some errand.

Some women flatly refused to let their daughters learn to spin, because "if you learn, you'll have to do it." Obviously such a woman hoped that her daughter would become other than a fisherman's wife. Other girls did not learn to spin because they went further in school than did the majority. At the time in their lives when most girls would be learning how to spin, they were attending school and studying for examinations. When I mentioned to Aubrey Pearce that my mother did not spin, he simply said, "But she was a teacher", in a tone of voice which seemed to indicate that there were some occupations a teacher did not have to take up.

After the wool was spun, it was twisted, i.e., two of the spun threads were twisted together to make a two-ply wool. Then it was put in "hanks," i.e., skeins and washed carefully. It was rolled loosely into balls from this stage. Then it was all ready for knitting. Women in Elliston did not dye their wool, but sometimes for variety they might mix black and white strands together. However the finished wollen garment might be dyed. For instance, girl's long stockings were knitted of fine white yarn, but when completed were then dyed black.

All the females in a household knitted, from the youngest schoolgirl to the elderly grandmother, since people wore lots of hand-knitted woolen garments, both inner and outer. A variety of knitted garments was required not only for use by all family members during blustery winter weather, but also for the summer use of the males who went fishing.

In the early 1900s many men wore knitted underwear in the summer as well as in the winter. This was lined with "fleece calico" which kept it from being itchy and irritable next to the skin. My maternal grandfather, Joseph Tilley, a man who weighed well over 200 pounds, was one of those who believed "what will keep out the cold will keep out the heat." It was probably his woolen underwear that made him exclaim one July day: "Tis a thousand in the shade". My father's generation still used long underwear in winter and also in summer while working on the water. Both seasons' clothing were store-bought then, the winter's clothing being a heavier weight than the summer's.

The basic items that most women had to knit included: knitted petticoats; long stockings, above the knee for women and girls, below the knee for men and boys; "vamps" (ankle height socks) for everyone in the family, as these were worn over regular stockings, especially in the rubber boots (waders): "cossocks,' a sort of helmet which covered the whole head and most of the face except the eyes, which was especially welcomed by those who went in the country ten to twelve miles for wood on snowy, frosty days in winter; mittens, which had a thumb and fore finger; cuffs, which had all fingers together with thumb only separate; gloves for dress wear; and possibly a "splitting mitt." Each family member needed three or four pairs of stockings, mitts and cuffs, for snow got into winter boots and mitts and cuffs were easily mislaid.

The largest garment that most women knitted from the 1920s onward was the "spun-yarn" sweater or "guernsey." Fishermen wore these, winter and summer, even in the 1940s. Women followed no written patterns, yet they turned out garments that fitten perfectly. I failed to ask how they managed to do this. They did not even use a measuring tape. I recall my mother using her middle finger as a measure and giving the length of a stocking leg as being so many "fingers" long instead of inches long.

Unattached younger women did a great deal of knitting for the family, but they also had time to do "fancy work." Embroidering cushion tops on "huckaback" (a material with raised loops available in the early 1900s), crocheting, and knitting lace, were fashionable occupations in the early days. In the 1930s and 1940s members of this age group were more interested in working with coloured thread, embroidering pillow slips, table cloths, aprons, and bedspreads. Nobody said they had embroidered any item. They simply said "I worked it."

Nearly every woman, unless she was hopeless with a needle, made most of her family's clothing, even as late as the thirties. Children's clothing especially was practically all homemade or made by local seamstresses. There were a number of women in Elliston who were classed as dressmakers. They were in great demand for doing tricky jobs such as cutting over an adult's cast-off garment and making it into something for a child, or for "turning" a coat for any family member, so that it might last another season (that is, they reversed the garment entirely, putting the faded part inside.) They did their work without benefit of any "bought" patterns. Few of them could have followed written instructions very well anyway.

Men's suits were either made by a tailor in Bonavista in earlier days or were bought ready-made. Women rarely attempted to make men's suits, although nearly every other article of their clothing was handmade at home in the early days. For instance, during the depression year of the 1930s men's top shirts were sometimes made from bleached flour sacks and were dyed the desired colour with "dolly dye" (store-bought dye.)

Most of the material used for clothing — broadcloth, flannel, serge, and cotton — could be bought in the local stores or at Bonavista. Sometimes, too, in the early 1900s, peddlers called at the door with material suitable for skirts and dresses. One informant recalled that on one occasion, when the peddler called at her home, an old man from the North Side was there too. His home had already been visited by the same peddler, and he said that he had bought some material from the peddler "to make a 'tail' for . . . " (that is, a skirt).

No matter what material she used, the sewer tried to make the finished item as nice as possible. Little girls' clothes especially had "deckers" (several rows) of ruffles. Flour sacking, used by poorer families for clothing, was widely used in all families in Elliston for pillow slips, aprons, table cloths, dish towels, and even sheets. Much bleaching made the material linenlike in appearance. All of these flour sack items were brightened by embroidery, and the women who grew up during the late twenties and early thirties were more adept with the embroidery needle and coloured cottons than they were with the crochet hool used by an earlier generation. The coloured thread was inexpensive and with a bit of skill and a few hours' work plain flour sacking was made very attractive.

29

Quilt-making or "joining quilts" was also considered a "winter job." Sometimes women managed to buy "burney" (shop soiled cotton material) cheaply and cut this in suitable pieces to make the quilt. Often though, they just cut up any old garment they had at home and any remnants. They chose an old flannelette sheet or blanket to "join the quilt on." Sometimes pieces were joined to, ie., sewn to, both sides of the sheet. Then the quilt was reversible. Othertimes they lined the quilt with a different material. Often "they used damask cotton, like they used for the big aprons worn then," Orpah Crewe told me. Most women made their quilts on their own. It was not the practice in Elliston to have "quilting parties" such as took place in the United States and England.

Hooking mats was another occupation reserved for wintertime. Sometimes a woman would hook several during the course of a winter and might "have one in the frame" to work on as a variation from knitting, or sewing.

The "mat frame" on which a mat was hooked consisted of four pieces of wood about 1″ thick, 2″ wide and any desired length. These pieces were joined together in a rectangle, but the fourth piece was moved into different slots in the side pieces as the work progressed. The mat was worked in sections, and as it was done it was rolled up so that the incompleted portion stayed taut in the frame.

A piece of brin was used for the backing, and as there were no transfers or ready bought patterns available, any design had to be drawn freehand in pencil. The variety of designs they made was astonishing — geometric, scrolls, flowers, animals. I remember one in our kitchen that featured a big black dog. A woman who was good at sketching would help a less skillful neighbour who could not draw as well. Very likely the neighbour reciprocated by doing something else for her. They used scraps of material or "rags" to form their patterns. Material was cut in long narrow strips and wound up in a ball. Good hookers tried to keep the size of the rags uniform. No old garment was ever thrown away, for if it could not be used in a quilt, it found a place in the rag rug. If a housewife did not have enough of a certain colour, she would dye white or light material the colour she desired. In the old days they used natural dyes for colouring rags. William Crewe said:

> I can remember when they used to go down and pick the rock moss and render it out and get the colour for the mats. They used to do that for to "fill 'em out" you know. (i.e., the background colour).

30

The rock moss used was the greyish-green scaly lichen which is found in abundance on the big rocks in the area. "They'd boil it away till it steeped out good . . . " said Mr. Crewe and "then they put their rags in," added his wife. The colour obtained by this process was a "barky" colour, a light rust-brown. In later years women used the dye they could buy in the shops. Mrs. Crewe said:

> We used to dye to get the right colours for the flowers in our mats, but they don't do that now. They gets the right colours.

For hooking the mat, that is, drawing up the rags through the spaces in the brin, they used a "mat hook." This was a straight piece of metal (sometimes copper) about 2″ long and set in a wooden handle. There was a small crook at the end for drawing up the loops. As with other crafts, women varied in their ability to hook mats. Some were acknowledged experts and took great pride in their work. Their loops were drawn up evenly and the inner side of the mat was free from blemishes. Such a mat could easily be reversed and few could notice the difference.

In the early days when many families had dogs for hauling firewood, the dog's tackling or harness was often made by the women of the household. Rope, string and cloth were used in making such a harness.

Even some of the woman's indoor work in late winter was directly involved with the fishery. Many women made sails in the days when all fishing boats were sailboats; sails were made and used up to and after the First World War. Men usually "cut out" the sails and roped them after they were made, i.e., attached the rope for raising and lowering the sail, but the women did the necessary sewing. Noah Chaulk remembered his mother making sails by hand for their fishing boat. For working by hand there was a special "sail needle" (triangular instead of round) and a "sail palm" made of leather with a round metal section for forcing the needle through the heavy material. Sails were made of cotton duck, a heavy canvas-like material. The finished sail was "barked" or "tarred" to strengthen it and increase its ability to hold the wind. Noah's wife Sarah remembered her mother making sails too, but she used a hand machine for the job.

It was a rare man indeed who did any work for his wife in the house, even though women often did men's work outdoors. A man would say, and truthfully, that he "never knew where anything was in the house." And, if his wife did not put out his clothing for him to wear, he would not know where to find it.

31

To be a good wife for a fisherman, a woman had to be versatile and prepared to work hard. In summer, her day could take her from house, to stable, to garden, to meadow, to stage, to flake. In fall, her days were taken up with picking berries, harvesting crops, making preserves, cleaning house, preparing for Christmas, and doing the preliminary preparations for making wool. In winter, carding, spinning, and knitting wool, sewing clothes, joining quilts and hooking mats were all done indoors. The woman had little leisure time, for in addition to having to pull her weight at a variety of jobs, she had to see to it that her family was properly fed and cared for. A man whose wife was competent in all these areas was rich, not only because she managed her household well, but also because of her real contribution to the economy of that household.

# Chapter 3
## Girlhood: The Learning Years

### WORK

Girls in Elliston during the period 1900–1950 were not long past baby-hood before they began to learn women's work and make a very real contribution to the work for the household. Both boys and girls in this period demonstrated the truth of the old adage "Children are a poor man's wealth," but girls had a multiplicity of duties both outdoors and indoors. Girls learned early that

> "A poor man works from sun to sun,
> But a poor woman's work is never done."

Both boys and girls did outside chores ("jobs," in Elliston), but a seasonal distinction was usually made. If a job involved brute strength or physical hardship such as braving snow, cold, or high winds, it was considered boys' work; otherwise it was girls' work. In summer, for instance, girls were expected to bring the vegetables from the root cellar, but on a stormy winter day it became a boy's job. In summer when animals roamed freely, they were the responsibility of the girls and women, who did the milking of cows and goats; but during the winter boys or men were responsible for the stabled animals.

Children of either sex were expected to "run messeges" for the older members of the family. They might borrow a cup of sugar from a neighbour, get a forgotten pipe for father, or carry verbal messages from the house to the work area "down below". Either boys or girls might be asked to bring in a supply of wood for the kitchen stove.

But housework was clearly girls' work. It was they who set the table, washed the dishes, swept the floor, rocked the baby, and so on. Generally speaking, boys did not do such chores if there were girls around. The prevailing attitude was something like that Campbell found among the Southern Highlanders in the United States: inside the house the girls were at the beck and call of the males.[1] In Elliston I have observed that if one of the men wanted a drink of water, a girl was expected to fetch it. This was acceptable if the request or order came from an adult or from someone engaged in a task; but it was rarely well-received by a girl if it came from a young brother lolling at his ease in the kitchen. In fact, unless the girl had a tight rein on her temper, such a request might lead to a fight.

It was not, however, the ordinary everyday tasks that my women informants remembered as being their first "real" jobs in the house. The ones that stood out in their memories were those which were done on a specific day of the week, or which required a special skill. The "milestones of activity" in the week included special Saturday jobs, like scrubbing the outside threshold, polishing family footwear in preparation for Sunday, and cleaning cutlery for Sunday use. Making bread, which might be done on any day of the week except Sunday, required a special skill, and a little girl was highly commended if her first batch turned out well. Several women commented specifically on each of these tasks.

My Aunt Hilda said that she did her first real job in the house between the ages of three and four. She was set to scrub the outside threshold (doorstep) with sand and a sprucebough scrubbing brush. This was a very responsible job for one so young, when one considers that in the early 1900s and even in the 1930s, the attitude of the housewife towards cleanliness might be measured by the whiteness of the threshold. Most women in Elliston were so careful about their thresholds that they would not use the same cleaning water for them as they used for the rest of the floor. They got a fresh lot of water so that the bare wood would show white and not "muddly" (a tattle-tale grey colour). Thresholds, although painted every spring or fall and sometimes both, soon lost their protective covering after weekly assaults from the scrubbing brush. Eventually one would become so worn it would have to be replaced.

One of the anecdotes my father used to tell when I was a child was about a man in Elliston who needed to replace a "drashel." He was not a carpenter so he asked for advice from his neighbour. He was told to make it a bit longer than the old one, and when he had taken out the old doorstep, to force the new wood in its place. This he did; but he was too forceful and in the process ruined the doorway.

The women of most households were expected to see that the family's Sunday clothes were in order by Saturday evening. The task of attending to the footwear, especially fathers' and brothers' boots, belonged to the younger girls, or to the only girl in the family. The boots had to be well-shined for Sunday — no "half measures" allowed. This tradition lingered into the 1940s, for I remember it was my job to get the Sunday shoes ready on Saturday.

In the days before the introduction of stainless steel, most girls were faced on Saturday with another time-consuming chore: the weekly cleaning of the family cutlery. The knives, forks, and spoons were cleaned with a substance called "bath-brick" In the early days, this was a solid block from which portions were chipped off; by the 1940s bathbrick would be bought in powder form in a tin. A soft rag was moistened, dipped in the powder, and then applied vigorously to the cutlery. Knives used to be given extra special attention; they were rubbed on a special board to give them a high polish. During my childhood, we no longer rubbed knives on a board.[2] The most frustrating side of this job was the knowledge that when the cutlery had been used once, it was almost as bad as ever. But at least the housewife had the satisfaction of knowing that they had been polished for the Sunday meals.

These tasks were also described as Saturday chores in the book *Lark Rise to Candleford*, which takes place in Oxfordshire, England, towards the end of the nineteenth century. Flora Thompson says: "Even the wives of carpenters and masons paid a girl sixpence to clean the knives and boots and take out the children on Saturday."[3]

Nearly all my elderly female informants mentiond "making" or "mixing" bread when they were quite young. Usually for their first attempts they had to stand on a kitchen stool to be tall enough to do the mixing, but by the time they reached the age of twelve, most of them were as skilled as their mothers in bread-making.

These first real jobs were all indoor tasks; but girls at a very early age had outside duties to attend to during all seasons of the year, except perhaps on stormy days in winter when boys did most of the outside work. In early spring, before the grass had grown very high, children and women were expected to "pick" the grass ground. They had to go over the meadow land inch by inch, picking up stones or any other debris that might have collected on the field during the winter. This custom had died out by the 1940s, at any rate I do not recall ever going "rock-picking."

Often when snow covered the fields and fences, short cuts or "snow paths" were taken across anyone's land. After the spring rock-picking all this changed. No one dared so much as disturb a blade of grass with a footfall; the men were very particular about the condition of the grass they cut. They did not relish the thought of scything trampled-over grass. Every blade counted if you wanted to keep several goats or cows over the winter, and oats were expensive. To my knowledge no one grew oats in Elliston, though I understand they were grown further north in Newfoundland. Oats were bought at the store in "oat sacks." These, I recall, were quite large bags and the sacking was of a different texture than other brin bags.

Even in the 1940s the attitude toward walking on unmown grass still prevailed. How fearful we children were when we crossed the "midder" to reach the spot where the "dewberries" grew, lest we place a foot out of the narrow path and be criticized by father or uncle. Said the lady who told me of her experience rock-picking: "Dare the child to go into a garden after the ground was picked."

Gardening was mainly the responsibility of the women and girls. Long before she was a teenager a girl worked alongside her mother and older sisters at the various tasks in the garden. Men attended to the ploughing or digging of the land devoted to potatoes, but smaller plots perhaps less than 20', x 20', used for the "small seeds", carrots, parsnips, beets, and cabbage, were looked after entirely by the women; that included the digging. My Aunt Hilda remembered having to dig the cabbage patch in the evening after coming home from school. She was eleven or twelve at the time, and she and her elder sister dug it twice over with their long-handled pointed shovels before Grandmother Chaulk considered it in proper shape to receive the cabbage plants.

Weeding was a chore girls attended to as soon as they knew the difference between a weed and a vegetable. Rarely, in the early 1900s, did men help with the weeding. This backbreaking job was for women. Aunt Hilda recalled how she, her sister, and a girl friend, lightened their weeding in the potato garden one summer. While two of them weeded steadily, the third one read a story book aloud to them. She did not say what their strict mother would have thought of this shirking of work.

I remember weeding the garden when I was quite young. As the only girl in the family, I had to work alone or with my mother. She taught me

36

the names of the various weeds, and showed me how to grasp them so as to pull them out of the potato bed without disturbing the potato plants. It was quite satisfying to look back over the work you had done knowing you would not have to do that again for the season.

Another outdoor job which fell to the girls' lot in mid- or late-June in the early 1900s was curing caplin. "Caplin scull" occurred at that time: the little, silvery-bellied six inch caplin "struck in" (came ashore to spawn). The cornmeal-like spawn seemed to be everywhere. I have vivid memories of men of Maberly "casting" caplin in the beach called "The 'Ire Mine," named for the rusty-red colour of the rocks over which a small stream trickled, and also in the cove where Muddy Brook enters the sea. Tall men like 'Lige (Ellijah) Pearce could throw the heavy-weighted, circular castnet effortlessly. Since each man held a corner of his castnet in his mouth before making a throw, denture wearers removed their dentures. Otherwise, the false teeth went flying with the net — great fun for the onlookers, but a serious matter for the loser. Down went the net in the midst of the school and was hauled in filled with the wriggling fish. A flick of the hand and the "bullets," which weighted the edges of the net, parted, releasing the fish into a natural depression in the rocks or in a prepared rock "pound." Children enjoyed the caplin casting because although they might have to work carrying the fish in buckets from the pound to the garden or stage, it was "play-work."

During the first years of the century nearly every household that did not have a horse kept several dogs. Their chief function during the winter was to haul the year's supply of firewood, and for this hard work they needed to be well-fed. Only the well-to-do kept dogs for pets. The chief diet for all dogs was dried, salted caplin. When Aunt Hilda was little her family had several dogs. She recalled that her brothers would cast the caplin before they left for a full day's fishing on the fishing grounds, taking what they needed for bait. These caplin for winter use were cured in salt for a day or two and then spread to dry. On one occasion when she was five or six years old, Aunt Hilda worked side by side with her older sister and mother from early morning to late afternoon spreading the salted caplin on the flake to dry. Grandmother Chaulk was very particular about how the little fish were spread. They had to be laid out straight and flat on the boughs — no crooked caplin allowed. Yet caplin were not often eaten by humans. One season, she said, they cured four puncheons of caplin; since one puncheon equals four barrels and one barrel equals two hundred pounds (cured caplin), the number of caplin the women handled was tremendous.

Aunt Hilda also recalled curing dogfish and flatfish (flounder) for the dogs. I used to think that the baby dogfish was rather cute, a miniature shark swimming along with its milk supply attached; but I know fishermen loathed the sight of the rough-skinned fish though they sometimes brought them ashore as food for the dogs. Flounder, considered a delicacy now, was rated as dogfood when I was growing up. I still retain my reluctance to eat it. My brothers and, I guess, generations of boys before them, sat in the boats tied up at the stagehead and stabbed the flatfish as they glided along the cove bottom. Whether people bothered to salt dogfish and flatfish before drying them I do not know.

At any time during the fishing season when there was a lot of dry (almost cured) fish on the flake and "it was working up" (rain was imminent), boys and girls were pressed into service on the flake. Everyone was expected to pitch in to get the fish taken up in faggots or the bigger "piles" (rectangular or circular) before the rain came. The children could not carry as many fish at a time as an adult, but they could make many trips and could arrange the fish in yaffles for the adults to carry to the pile or the faggot. These would be covered with spruce "rinds" (bark) held down with heavy rocks.

When young children were engaged in this work they were under parental supervision and were not in mischief or danger elsewhere. Children, at least some children, enjoyed the sense of being part of the work team and working to defeat the elements. The same attitude prevailed at the haymaking. A child who raked cleanly, leaving no wisps of hay behind, was praised. I recall many times in my childhood rushing from flake to meadow, working against time to get things done. But it wasn't all rush, rush, rush. Usually we worked at a steady rate and when work was finished there was time for a chat. Those I enjoyed most were the ones when my Aunt Beck (Rebecca) spoke of her first years in Maberly and the pranks she played on the older women of the community. I was fascinated by her stories; they cast her in a role quite different from the one I saw her in.

Another outdoor activity both boys and girls engaged in was berry-picking, children accompanied their parents to the "berry-hills" or "barrens" for blueberries and partridge berries. When they grew older, girls would often go berry-picking in groups of four or five. Boys tended to be more solitary and ranged further afield in search of a good "patch." Rarely did mixed groups of boys and girls go berry-picking unless they went as a family group. However, different groups might pick berries in the same area and "boil the kettle" together, that is, have lunch together. Blueberries were picked before partridge berries so everyone kept on the lookout for good patches of partridge berries as they gathered the blueberries. Children's nimble fingers could gather many gallons of berries so large families could do well on "the berries" if they fetched a fair price. ($1.00 a gal.). Thus many older children did not attend school during September, but started in October, having earned enough "off the hills" to supply them with their winter's clothing.

Later in the fall, most young girls had to help their mothers "picking the wool." Two or three of the women I talked with told me they used to do this in the evening after they had attended to their school work. They were expected to go through the previously washed wool and remove all the foreign matter, twigs, grass, etc., before it was carded.

By the time she reached the age of ten, a girl in most households was contributing to the regular round of work. In the early days she might even go "into service" in another home to look after small children while the mother was "down below" doing stage and flake work. Rarely would she be expected to do much in the line of heavy household tasks at this age; her chief duty was to supervise the younger child or children so that the busy housewife might be free to do her many outside chores. Usually young girls were in service with people they knew in the nearby communities or in the same community. They rarely worked in strangers' homes.

In certain exceptional cases girls did women's work, for instance, after losing a parent. One woman, whose mother died when she was just a small girl, spent her winters, when her father was working away from the community, with either her aunt or older married sister. The first job she remembered as special was making bread at her aunt's home. She was nine years old at that time and had to stand on a stool to do the mixing. Her uncle praised her first effort by remarking to his wife: "Far better than yours." Very early in life she had to assume the woman's role, for she was the only girl in the family left now at home. Not only did she do the housework, but she also had to do a woman's work in the stage and on the flake. She was allowed to go to school during the winter until she finished grade two. At that point her father decided she was educated enough and kept her out of school although she wanted to stay.

By the age of ten, she was working side by side with her aunt "down below" for her father and his brother fished together. One of her chores was to carry the "washed out" fish from the stage to the flake on a handbar, a job which in some fishing crews was done by the men as it was considered too heavy work for women. Her aunt held up one end of the bar and she the other. One morning the bridge to the flake was slippery and, in addition, there were too many fish on the bar. She fell and broke her wrist. A neighbour, using a piece of sailcloth for the bandage and hoops from a fish tub for splints, attended to her wrist. He did a good job. Canon Bayly, the Anglican parish priest and an acknowledged authority on all matters, pronounced it a good job. She never did see a doctor about it and the wrist healed perfectly. Her regular job in the stage at that time, and for some years, was "cutting throats." But she also had to take part in several other operations connected with handling the fish, including bringing them in "tubbars" (200 pounds or more at a time) from the stagehead to the splitting area.

Should her father have fish to put away on Tuesday evening, however, she was usually excused. It was customary for Canon Bayly to hold church services in Maberly, winter and summer, on Tuesday evenings at seven o'clock. Although a Methodist, she tried to attend every service. A boy from next door would take her place in the stage unless he himself had to work at his father's fish. Hers, of course, was an exceptionally difficult childhood, but there were undoubtedly others.

Another who had a difficult childhood was an eighty-one year old woman whose father was lost "on the ice" near Elliston when she was about ten years old. Her mother had to bring up both the girl and her younger brother practically without help. The widow's "mite" in those days was a "mite" indeed — $4.00 every quarter from the government. Before the girl had reached her teens she had started to work for a woman who was a practical nurse in the community. This woman had no training, but she did have a "doctor's book" and a great desire to help others. Wherever there was sickness, she was there to render what help she could, and her "servant girl" usually accompanied her on her rounds.

"Aunt" Betsy remembered standing on a block to do the family washing by hand, and making bread before she was twelve years old. She was also doing a regular maid's work, including bringing the daily supply of water for the household from the public well, a quarter to a half a mile away, with an extra amount on washdays. In the summer, she was expected to work at the grass and weed the vegetables. Since the service period was normally from May to the end of October, she probably managed to go to school most of the winter. At any rate she reached Grade IV. She married at seventeen.

When I asked about early jobs, few of the women whom I talked to mentioned knitting, sewing and darning, perhaps because they did not consider these activities as household tasks. Yet nearly all girls could knit by the time they were seven or eight years old, and most of them had started at four or five years of age, just as the girls did in old New England.[4] In Elliston, one of the complicated items a girl would be expected to knit, after learning "garter stitch," i.e., plain knitting on a head band or garters, was a pair of long stockings for herself, or, perhaps a "splitting mitt" for her father. In my childhood the same system prevailed. I learned to knit while I was quite young, perhaps eight or nine. I wore the "cable-stitch" cardigan that I had knitted during the fall when I was twelve for the first time at that year's Christmas concert.

At about the same time that she learned how to knit, a girl was also taught how to handle a sewing needle. She was expected to be able to sew on buttons, to hem, and to sew up rents in clothing, especially her own. Unless they showed unusual aptitude, it is doubtful that very young girls did much more than such necessary plain sewing, at least until they were teenagers.

Because they used wool from their own sheep, with no additives to lengthen the wearing period, items like knitted stockings soon became thin at points of stress, that is, at heel and toe. Hence girls had to master the secret of darning fairly soon. Not only did they have to keep their own hosiery in a state of repair, but as they became more skillful they would be expected to look after this side of the family mending. A girl who could darn well was said to darn a hole "as if it were woven"; there were no missed strands and the work was done neatly and evenly. A darn that was roughly and carelessly done was termed "just a brail" and was the sign that the darner took no pride in her work.

Girls had to learn how to knit and sew when they were quite young since a great deal of the family's clothing was homemade in the early 1900s. Knitting the stockings and mittens for a large family was a monumental task; the carding and spinning of that much wool was just as time consuming. A woman with a dozen boys in her family and no daughter must have relied on outside help.

A little girl of the early 1900s, like her mother and older sisters, wore ankle-length dresses winter and summer. And, to protect the dress she wore either a "pinafore" or a "bib apron." A pinafore hung from the shoulders with a yoke, the lower part gathered with ruffles at the armholes. Often they were made of "pretty cotton" (probably floral print). When they were made of shirting (very likely white), they were trimmed

41

with lace. A bib apron was always ruffled and trimmed with lace. Orpah Crewe remembered wearing "pinnys" or "pinafores" over her dress when she went to school. She had two; thus her mother could manage to provide her with a clean starched pinny for each school day. Aunt Hilda also said: "We wore pinafores as soon as we could walk."

A pre-teen's other clothing was very little different from an older girl's garments. However, as my Aunt Hilda explained, she was not encased in "restrictive" clothing till she started to develop. In winter, up until about twelve years of age, she wore a flannelette chemise. This was a rather shapeless garment simply having round holes cut in a straight piece of material for the neck and the short sleeves. Then there were pants or bloomers, again of flannelette with elastic at the knees. Stockings were knitted from homespun yarn. These were done of fine white wool, but the finished item was dyed black. These stockings reached way above the knee and were held up either by knitted garters or more often by a band of cotton as the knitted garters often were not tight enough. She wore two flannelette petticoats, and the top "undergarment" was a camisole which closed at the waist with buttons. Winter dresses were of heavy cloth, such as flannel. The mittens, knitted of spun yarn were dyed bright colours. Caps were woolen, too and probably matched the mittens, but I failed to check this. Said Aunt Hilda: "We did not feel the cold too much about our heads as we had lots of hair."

During the summer on weekdays girls wore sunbonnets made of shirting; but they had hats for church and Sunday school. Some of the hats were made of silk, but more often of straw. Unlike the other clothing, hats were not made at home. One woman said: "I liked the sailor hat with streamers down the back, nearly all had streamers." The footwear, of very heavy leather for wintertime, and supposedly watertight with soles put on with wooden pegs instead of nails, was made in Elliston. There were three practising shoemakers in the community during the early part of the century. Winter coats were of some heavy material: "It seemed at least a quarter inch thick" said one woman. Around her neck a girl might wear a wool boa. This "was like a sheep's tail, but long enough to go twice around the neck and tied with a piece of ribbon below the chin," Said Aunt Hilda: "It felt so cosy, [I] was quite dressed up when I got a new one about every two years."

In the summertime all of the homemade clothing was of lighter material than the winter flannelette. Chemises, petticoats (still two in number), pants, etc., were usually made of shirting. Petticoats would be trimmed with lace and perhaps had a ruffle or two. Stockings were worn in summer, but these were of a lightweight material. Aunt Hilda said, "Mother bought machine knit lengths, cut the length desired, and toes were knitted on them." Boots were worn; old winter ones for everyday wear, but "laced boots made of lovely kid" for Sundays. Summer dresses were made of cotton for everyday wear, but for "best" they chose lawn, a very fine material. Another material used was "nun's veiling," which looked like chiffon. It was available in different colours but was not considered practical by most people who demanded durability for "best" clothes which were expected to last for years and years. Ordinarily girls did not have a coat for summer wear.

In the early 1900s every girl wore her hair long. Usually she wore a band or comb round it to keep it from falling forward at school, but at home it was braided and tied with a ribbon. In the 1940s hair styles varied, Not all girls wore their hair long. Girls who had thick straight hair often wore it cut short with a full bang over the forehead; locally they called this style "the French crap" or "crop". Others wore their hair over their shoulders; the hair was held back by hair clips or bands, or was braided and tied with a ribbon. The latter style was preferred during school hours for it offered less chance for a girl "to get something in her head" for, unfortunately, a few families did not consider lice to be dirt the way most families did. For special occasions, long straight hair was braided into numerous tiny plaits which were kept in overnight. The next day, when the plaits were undone and combed out, the child's hair was full of kinky waves.[5] I remember having my hair styled in this fashion for a day-long trip to Little Catalina when I was about ten or eleven years old.

By the thirties and forties, although many things had not changed in little girls' day-to-day living, fashions in clothing had changed. They still wore some homemade flannelette underclothing in winter, but most underwear could now be purchased in the local stores. And with the introduction of snow or ski pants in the forties, girls no longer had to wear the heavy, dark-blue, fleece-lined, gym style bloomers. Woolen stockings were still being worn but cotton or lisle (even for winter wear) were being used, and in summer, girls wore ankle socks. For everyday wear in winter, most girls wore long, knee-length rubber boots like their brothers wore. But for "best wear," both girls and boys wore rubber overshoes over their regular shoes and boots. The boys' overshoes or "gaiters" had clasps to close them, but the girls' were usually "pull-ons" called "Russian Rubbers." Low shoes, usually the stodgy laced-up variety, were worn most of the time during the summer and fall, although for rough playing, especially "in the beach," "shucks" (rubber waders cut off at the ankle) were favoured by many girls and boys. Cotton dresses were normal everyday wear in summer and it was still customary for a girl to have a best dress for Sunday and special occasions. However, unlike the little girl who grew up during the first decades of the century, the girl of the forties was not hampered by her skirt which was knee length

Certainly, because of the girls' contribution to the work of the household: in growing and preparing food, in making and repairing clothing, very few of them ever had to be admonished for being wasteful. What A.M. Earle says of colonial children was also true of children in Elliston:

> Children . . . knew the value of everything in the household, knew the time it took to produce, for they had laboured themselves, and they grew to take care of the small things, not to squander and waste what they had so long been at work on.[6]

These values were further emphasized during teenage and young adulthood.

### PLAY

In spite of their restrictive style of dressing, at least during the early 1900s, and their many daily tasks, girls still found time for many kinds of recreational activity. For the children of Elliston during the period 1900-1950, the roadside, the "drungs" (narrow lanes between gardens), under the flakes, and brooks and "steadies" (where a brook widens out and deepens), the cliffs, and the beach, were the playgrounds. Grass ground, enclosed by fences, was forbidden territory in summer.

Each generation in Elliston shared some of the same ideas about animals, insects, birds and plants as those held by children in Britain and America. For instance, the belief that if a child lost a tooth outdoors and a dog swallowed it, a dog's tooth would grow in the child's mouth, persisted even in the 1940s. Consequently, most children made very sure that all baby teeth were thrown in the kitchen fire. No child in the community had heard of putting one's tooth under the pillow so that the kind fairy would leave some money in exchange. They shared the healthy respect accorded dragonflies, although in Elliston the name "dragonflies" was unknown. These harmless insects were called "arse-stingers," "horse-sting-

44

ers" or "hoss stingers." Children believed that they could be badly stung by one of these.[7] The beneficial reddish centipede was also feared. It was called an "earwig" or "yurwig" and no child liked to lie down for a nap outdoors in case one of these crawled in his ear.[8]. The fat, greasy, loathesome slugs that were abundant among the dew-dampened grass of early morning or after a wet spell were addressed thus:

Beaverthorn, put out your horns,
The cows are in your garden.[9]

Beaverthorn or "baverthorn" was the local name for slugs.

Ants carrying eggs, which happened when their nest was disturbed, were termed "emmets with their puddings."

Birds were plentiful in the early days of the century when the woods came right down to the settlement. By the 1950s there were fewer birds, but one, the crow, was still very much in evidence. In the old days it was looked upon with dislike by most girls. Even today my informants say they do not like to see crows. They could give no reason for the dislike, but two women I talked to said that when they were children, if they saw a crow about to cross their path, they would immediately turn their backs to it. Children in the 1940s, as far as I know, had no special dislike for crows.

Plants and wild flowers were often used by Elliston children during playtime as toys. In summertime, clumps of rushes grew by the brooks. These rounded green stalks could be twisted and woven together to make all sorts of items: handles, small baskets, whips, and canes. A shrill, ear-piercing whistle could be produced by placing a broad blade of grass between the thumbs and blowing on it. A broad iris leaf with its top bent back and held in place by a tiny stick, made a grand little boat to sail on the smooth surface of a pond or a steady. Buttercups, too, grew in profusion, but they were not played with as were the dandelions: perhaps because they were more likely to be found on the fenced-in grassground. Dandelion stems were just the thing for making chains to encircle waists, necks, wrists, and ankles; but they were rarely called dandelions. To many they were the "piss-a-beds" and to others less "vulgar" they were "totties". Even when dandelions had lost their yellow petals, they were still played with. A child would blow as hard as he could to send the umbrella-like seed flying in the air. But I have not heard any saying or rhyme connected with this action.

45

When girls picked the white field daisy or bachelor's button, they often plucked the petals repeating the following formula: "He loves me/He loves me not/A little/Not much/Sincerely/To the Heart." Flowers were also used in some of their Midsummer ceremonies. It was the custom for two girls, working together, to gather "cliff flowers" which grew in profusion from the cracks in the sides of the cliffs. They planted three of them in a row in a special secret spot on Midsummer Eve. The middle flower represented the girl; those on either side were named for two boys she had a liking for. In the morning, if one of these had drooped towards the middle flower it meant that that boy had a liking for her.

Elliston children did not have access to cultivated varieties like hollyhock or columbine or pansies for few families kept flower gardens. They had to play with wild flowers only.[10]

Besides the flower rites, little girls had other means of finding out who they were going to marry. The buttons on one's outside clothing would be counted thus: "Tinker, tailor, soldier, sailor, rich man, poor man, prodigal, thief." Some said "beggerman" instead of "prodigal," but the rest of the rhyme was the same. Because this was a community also wedded to the sea it is not strange that little girls were most pleased when their buttons worked out to "sailor." No one wanted a thief. If a girl were eating an apple she might take three seeds and name each for a boy she liked. These she placed on the hot stove. The one that jumped first was the one who cared the most. Other love divinations were peculiar to Midsummer's Day and no other time. These were practiced chiefly by girls of marriageable age and will be dealt with in the next chapter.

In late spring and early summer before the grass grew high, many happy hours were spent in the "yard," "making gardens" with three- to four- inch high sticks for the "fence." These were laid out with lanes leading to gates etc., but nothing was planted in the enclosed area. Here they were imitating the adults having fences to protect their gardens and meadows. A play area used chiefly in spring and fall was a clearing among trees in a "farm," i.e., a woodlot. Here one could gather spruce buds to mix with rain water for ink. Girls liked to have "playhouses" or "cobyhouses" here, and often while playing in one of these areas near the school they would ignore the bell signalling the end of recess period and keep on with their play until dinnertime at noon. They did not worry about the "caning" they were sure to receive from the teacher in the afternoon.

Both boys and girls spent most of the summer playtime on the beaches or around the cliffs. Fenced-in meadows were forbidden areas in summer, and except for the roadsides there were open spaces only on the outskirts of the community. On the beach children found all sorts of interesting items. Aunt Hilda said that when she was a child in the early 1900s she used to pick up "fairy handbars." These were sections of seaweed tossed up on the beach which, when dry, resembled the handbar used for carrying fish. In the thirties and forties children picked up "oar's (whore's) eggs," the prickly sea urchin which, when dry, lost its spines and made a nice round coracle-type boat. They also pried small shells loose from the rocks at high water mark. These shells, less than an inch in diameter, were shaped very much like pointed Chinese peasant hats, and were called "ol' domans" (old womans). The gelatine-like substance inside the shell was forced out with a thumbnail and the empty shell set sailing in small salt water puddles among the rocks.

Of course girls also sailed boats in the salt water puddles but usually girls' boats were rough, often just shaped with an axe. However, they were content with this and each spring faithfully smeared them with paint when the family fishing boat got its new coat. My boat, which was of this variety, was further dressed up with a tin, orange and red "Better Beaver" tobacco tag on the bow. On the other hand some boys had very elaborate boats, complete in every detail. Such boats were rarely sailed in mere puddles. They were moored in at the steady or another deep place in the brook where the boys had special "collars" and wharves.

Girls often played "copyhouses," "cobyhouses," (i.e., playhouses) in the rocks just above the dash of the sea. When the time for wading arrived they would dabble in the sea, holding their skirts just above their knees. For parents, August first was the proper time for wading in the ocean, but children went any hot July day. Probably children stuck chiefly to the beach and cliffs play areas in summertime because here they were within call of the group working in the stage or on the flake and were ready to be called to perform any task they were capable of: for example, "boiling the kettle" for a "mug-up" — a light meal, or "lunch" consisting of bread and butter and hot tea. Usually there was also something for a "relish," like jam, cold fish, beans or cold meat.

It was unheard of for girls to go swimming in the early days. In Maberly the boys had their "swimmin' hole" but it was in a secluded part approached by a high cliff. Since no one possessed a bathing suit the boys probably swam in the nude. No girl would dream of going near the swimmin' hole. By the 1940s, Sandy Cove, situated between the Neck and Elliston Centre, was becoming increasingly important as a swimming area for

47

both sexes. How popular this beach was in the early days is a matter of conjecture for there were very few individuals who were in a position to loll around the beach for a number of hours during the daytime. However, with the coming of the Americans to the small base in Mark's Path during the Second World War, it became a favourite swimming spot. The soldiers spent many of their off-duty hours there during the summer. A favourite swimming place on the North Side of Elliston was a pond just behind the community, but it was probably only for boys.

It was the children themselves who ran their playtime hours. No grownups interfered or set down the rules; play was initiated by the children, run by the children, and enjoyment of the playing was the key — not the winning or losing. Most of the games required no set number of players; hence children could chose to play whatever their collective fancies turned to. Generally though, those activities which required more than two or three participants were only carried on when children were attending school. Summertime games usually involved only one or two individuals, for children had certain duties to attend to which kept them within hailing distance of their respective families.

Other activities might be indulged in by an individual on his own and had no season except that those often practiced indoors were thought of as winter activities. Most of these needed some equipment but nearly always homemade; for example, "blowing bubbles." This wasted soap and was messy so it was not particularly popular with parents, but it required no fancy equipment. No one had a special pipe for bubble blowing. Instead, an empty sewing-cotton reel (spool) was rubbed over the wet surface of the soap making a film over the hole in the centre. Then the child blew gently through the other hole and the bubble thus formed floated away, showing all the hues of the rainbow.

A bit of whittling by an older brother or father produced an excellent spintop from an empty sewing spool (plus a small pointed stick). Some little girls had lovely dolls' cradles and most girls had at least one store-bought doll (straw body but china head and arms and legs). Usually this was not played with every day being considered too precious to be soiled by grubby little hands. But probably most girls had home-made rag dolls for everyday use. I remember Aunt Hilda mentioning having one, but I can't remember having one myself. Some children also had tiny wheelbarrows and "flatcars" which were smaller copies of those used by older family members. A flatcar was made the same way as a wheelbarrow except it had no box; instead it had a flat slatted surface. A metal hoop from a barrel was often used for rolling. It was controlled by a piece of bent wire. Boys and girls nailed paint can lids to sticks and rolled them around. These didn't last long for the nail hole soon wore big even when one used a leather washer.

Other activities needed no equipment, just people willing to play. "Weighing butter" was a game which popped up now and then any time of the year and was more a physical excercise than a game. Two people stood back to back, hooking their arms together. Then, alternately, each bent, raising the other onto her back. Another favourite activity was for two people to sit on the floor or ground, the soles of their feet touching. Grasping a stick or bar between them they would rock back and forth. Called "Lazy Stick" this was really a test of strength. For "Goosie goosie gander" two girls would join hands facing each other. They would lean back with toes touching and would whirl around as fast as possible until one called out "stop." An individual might attain the same state of dizziness by holding onto an upright post with one hand and propelling himself round and round as fast as possible. "Skin the Cat" was considered a boys' activity, but girls indulged in it when they found a spot free from prying eyes. A player had to hang head-down from a high bar or rail and hold on by twisting his legs around the bar. While hanging on he had to remove his outer jacket or sweater without falling from his place. A girl who played this game was rated an "out-an-out tomboy."

One feature that all children's games had in common was that they could all be played without benefit of standard equipment. The things they used were a short piece of rope, a stick, a rock, stones or buttons. So with the exception perhaps of the game "Pitch the Buttons," play could begin on a moment's notice. Buttons used for pitching could be of any size, ranging from a two-inch coat button to a small pearl shirt button, and players started their first game of the season (usually spring) using buttons raided from their mother's "button can" where all buttons cut from worn out clothing were placed. A rock would be chosen across which the button had to be pitched — this process was termed "through the door." A certain spot had to be pitched for, and whoever came nearest was the winner, entitled to pick up all the losers' pitched buttons. It often happened that a skilful player would come home with his pockets bulging with buttons while the less skilful players might return home with many missing from their clothes. Losers probably "gained" a licking or a telling-off for their part in the game.

A game that girls played from spring until fall was "skipping rope."

Lily Pearce did not mention "skipping rhymes" but, while talking about her childhood in the early 1900s she said.

> And we'd have all kinds of games like that. I can remember about them. You'd sing, and while you'd be singing you'd be skipping. Perhaps you'd be washing your face, or combing your hair, or ironing your clothes. All sorts of actions you know.

I do not recall skipping to rhymes but shortly after my childhood they seemed to be popular.

"Jump the rope" was a favourite game of both sexes and was often played at recess time during the spring and fall. Two children would hold the rope stretched tightly between them at a certain height above the ground. Others would jump over this. The rope got raised higher and higher until all but one, who became the winner, was eliminated. Such jumping presented no problems to the tomboys of the 1940s with their short skirts, but girls of the early 1900s must have faced quite a problem with their long trailing skirts.

Another recess-time game which I remember playing and which was played also in the early 1900s was "Leap the frog." A number of children crouched down in a row. Each player had to go through the row jumping over the backs of the others and then herself had to assume a crouching position.

A game played at recess-time by young girls was "Little Sally Saucer." This was a ring game. One girl crouched in the centre and the others danced around her, hands joined. They sang:

> Little Sally Saucer, sitting in the water
> Weeping and crying for her young man.
> Rise up Sally, wipe away your tears,
> Point to the east, point to the west
> And choose the one that you love best.

As the words "point to the east, point to the west" were sung "Sally" would choose one to take her place. "It would go on from there until we became tired,"[11] said Aunt Hilda.

Girls also played "Here we go round the Mulberry Bush."[12] They sang:

> Here we go round the mulberry bush, the mulberry bush, the mulberry busy,
> Here we go round the mulberry bush

So early in the morning.

Then for each day of the week they chose an appropriate house- hold duty and performed the action, singing for Monday for instance:

This is the way we wash our clothes, wash our clothes, wash our clothes,
This is the way we wash our clothes,
So early Monday morning.

For Sunday they Sang:
This is the way we go to church, go to church, go to church,
This is the way we go to church,
Early Sunday morning.

Another singing game which they played at recess time in the early 1900s was "The Farmer in the Dell." No one described it to me. I presume it was played then as it was in the 1940s.

Hopscotch was a "girls-only" game, especially girls 8-13 years old. The playing area was usually outlined with a stick in the dusty road or in a gravelled section near the school. It looked something like this:

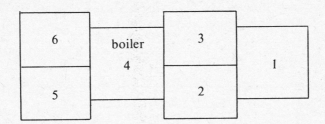

First some small object (a flat stone or a piece of glass) had to be pitched to land in square number one. A player was "out" if it touched a line or rolled out and landed anywhere but in the block aimed for. Then, hopping on one foot, a player had to hop in each square except the one in which the thrown piece lay. There could be no stepping on lines. On the return trip the piece was picked up and that square hopped in. Round completed, the player turned her back to the diagram and tossed her playing piece over her shoulder. Whichever square it landed in was "initialed" and could not be hopped in thereafter by anyone. The player attaining most "initials" was the winner.[13]

51

"Jackstones"[14] was a game played by girls during spring, summer, and fall. They usually played outside on a level grassy spot, using five smooth rounded stones. Girls were warned of the dire consequences should they sit on the grass-ground before it had warmed up sufficiently in the spring. My mother, to back up her warning, would relate how a little girl had "caught her death" from sitting on damp grass playing jackstones. Aunt Hilda had this to say:

> A great deal of our time was taken up, as soon as it was dry enough to sit on the grass, by playing marbles or jack stones, the latter chosen from the side of the roads, nice round ones. Five were used. We would take the five stones in our hands and toss them up, try to catch as many as we could on the back of our hand. We tossed them again and let them fall on the grass, pick up one, toss it up and try to pick up one from the grass, without touching another, and catch the one which was tossed. We did that until we had all four.

The four on the grass were picked up in groups of two. This was called "twos." "Threes" followed. A single stone was picked up and then three together. In "fours" all four stones had to be picked up while the tossed one was in the air and this had to be caught also. The game could be made more difficult by spacing the stones a great distance apart during the tossout. Aunt Hilda added:

> We also "drove the cows home." We spread our fingers apart and put a stone in the four spaces between the fingers and caught the tossed stone, something like juggling.

When you had completed all these actions you had won a game of jackstones. A dropped stone or one missed in the picking up meant you were "out" and it was another player's turn.

The game "cat" was played chiefly in the spring and fall. It was considered a boys' game but girls played it also. One informant, Lily Pearce, described it thus:

> We had a stick or something. Then you'd have a big stick in your hand and then you'd pick up another one a small one, you know, and chip toward that and see who could beat it off or something. We used to call that 'Cat'."

Edward Chaulk (Ned) described it differently:

> You'd dig a hole in the ground there and you'd go so far away and dig another one, and then you had a stick about that long (three-four feet), two hands (players). And one hand'd pitch the cat to them and they'd strike'n and the other fullor (fellow),'d pitch'n back and forth to the other fullor (fellow) and strike'n that way. Back and forth. You had the hole and you'd run when you'd get "cat". Whoever'd be to the hole first you'd be the game, get the game see. You'd run from one hole to the other see when you'd strike the cat you'd run and the other fullor'd be watching the cat and wouldn't be watching his hole and you'd get'n down see, and you'd get the game.[15]

I don't know the version of the 1940s for I did not play it myself.

"Duck on the Rock"[16] was also played by both boys and girls although it is generally considered a boys' game. Any number of players could take part. It stressed good markmanship. A big rock was an essential feature and on top of it was placed another smaller rock or a piece of stick. Each player stationed himself at a certain distance from the big rock and tried to "Bate 'n off," that is, knock off the small object, by throwing smaller rocks in turns. "Bate 'n off so many times you know, you'd be the beater see" (you'd win the game) said Edward Chaulk. This game was still popular in the 1940s.

The game called "Old Daddy" or "Oh Daddy"[17] was one which involved lots of running. Any number of players could take part and it was open to boys and girls from toddlers to teens. In the 1940s it used to be a favourite activity for mixed groups especially when they gathered in the early evening, spring through fall, but the older people I talked to did not mention this game. One player was chosen as "Daddy" and he was armed with a switch of some kind — a bough, a stick, or a piece of rope. One spot was designated as "home" where all players were safe. All players would venture out from home and taunt Daddy who would give chase, lashing out at all and sundry. Once someone was caught and hit by the switch, he had to be the "Daddy" in turn. Much of the fun of this game was the taunting and getting away with it.

In winter, snow was basic to outdoor play. "Riding" or "sliding" topped the list of play activities. Every section of the community had its favourite "riding spot" or spots. Since Maberly is located in a small valley with a brook running through it, there were several good slopes for riding on the Lane, the Big Hill, the hill by Pearces, the Midder, the Head. Neck children were not so fortunate since the main road through the community was fairly level. They often used "Government Hill," a big hill located perhaps half a mile inland from the The Neck. In Elliston Centre, the chief riding areas were on the main road through the town. Henry George's Hill and Joe Baker's Hill were two hills which converged on the Square and my mother, who came from Elliston Centre, often told of coming down one of these hills with momentum great enough to carry on right along the main road to the Dock on the Point. The North side had some good sliding areas too, but I cannot name particular ones as this section of the community is strange to me as I never went to that section of the community in my childhood. In spite of the proximity of most sliding areas to the seashore, there is no record of anyone's ever riding into the sea, though they did hit fences now and then.

Both in the old days and during the 1940s, the "slides" were homemade. Some children had to use the family "dog slide" (the big, heavy slide on which firewood was hauled by a team of dogs, rarely more than two dogs). Lucky children whose fathers were handy with axe and hammer had slides tailored to their size, especially for riding on. Everyone wanted the fastest slide and every effort was made to get the steel shoes on the runners as bright as possible. The hill would be crowded with girls and boys ranging from little tykes to gangling teenagers. The biggest or the bossiest was usually the steerer; he or she sat on the rear seat and guided the slide on its run down the slope only by the pressure of feet on the snow. This "skoating," as steering was called, was very hard on the footwear, whether the homemade leather boots of the old days or the long rubber boots of later years. Three people or more might share a slide. There would be a steerer on the back seat, a passenger on the front seat, and someone else crouched in the middle of the slide, feet on the runners and holding on the front "horns," in the "coucheying down" position. There might even be a fourth person standing on the runners behind the steerer. Often the course was made rougher by hollowing out ditches or pits over which the riders were expected to steer. Sometimes the level was raised in a certain spot so that a ridge went across the course. Either way the riders got a terrific jolt when crossing these obstacles, and there were even a few slides that "capsized" at these spots. Why someone wasn't killed I don't know. Usually there was competition, a race between riders. There was no competition but a different kind of excitement when seven or eight slides were joined in a row and started off down the hill. For this the fastest slide had to be placed at the head of the line with the slowest bringing up the rear. Otherwise the result would have been a colossal pile-up.

Sleds were also used but they were homemade, often by the boys themselves, and fashioned out of barrel staves. The sleek metal and wood ones only began to be used in the late 1940s. Few girls had sleds. If she were lucky, a girl might borrow her brother's sled for one or two rides.

Young children of both sexes enjoyed sliding over high snow drifts. Sometimes they sat on pieces of cardboard or smooth rocks, but often there was nothing but clothing in contact with the snow. This was hard on clothes, and girls who took part in this sport before the days of snow-pants must have been quite uncomfortable in a very short time.

Skating was not so popular in the period 1900–1950 as it is now. Few people had skates and until the late 1940s the most commonly used were the runners which fastened to one's ordinary footwear. For most children skating meant sliding, standing up, on an icy patch. One woman stated that she and her companions went skating but "we had no skates, just nails in our boots."

Girls and boys enjoyed making snow houses. A drift by a hillside was considered ideal for a large house. Sometimes they cooperated on a big snowhouse and crowned their efforts with a fire inside the chamber. Snow forts were constructed too, and there were fierce snow fights.

Often in March the Arctic ice packed in close to the shore. Then, in spite of parental objections, boys and girls went "copying pans," jumping from ice pan to ice pan as they floated on the sea. In Elliston this was an especially dangerous game. Aside from the fact that a "ducking" in very cold water was often the reward for the least clumsy move, a change of wind or tide could start the ice pack moving off shore pretty quickly and a "copyer" might find himself heading for the open Atlantic.

More than once a "copyer" had to be thrown a "longer" or "lunger" (sticks used to form the wooden platforms of the flakes or stages) to pole back to the shore. I remember this happening to my older brother, Albert, and I know it must have happened to others as well.

Children spent much of their spare time playing together, but frequently there were fights, and very rough ones, too. Several older men mentioned fighting a lot as children in the early 1900s. and I know the children of the 1940s, both boys and girls, spent nearly as much time fighting among themselves as they did playing together. Settling matters with our fists was part of our growing-up. Girls were told not to fight but that didn't deter us in the 1940s.

SCHOOLING

One might get the idea from the earlier part of this chapter that girls, because of their manifold household duties had an extremely rough, unpleasant life in Elliston. No doubt a few did, but the majority, like girls everywhere, had time for recreation too. Most important of all, they could attend school, for there is a long tradition of girls going to school in Elliston. That is why I dealt with the history of schools at such length in Chapter One, since the pattern of 1900–1950 was set in earlier days.

Governmental authorities realized quite early that the amount of schooling practicable for any child depended on her family's circumstances. Reports submitted to the government by early school inspectors give various reasons for the "moderate" advance of scholars in most parts of the island. The earliest report blamed it chiefly on the island-wide practice of employing child labour in the fishing industry. Later reports cited the extreme poverty of the parents and also parental indifference. Certainly poverty seems to have had a bearing on the schooling of children in the Maberly-Neck area. During the depression period of the Thirties no one in this section of the community completed high school; yet quite a number had done so prior to that period. By the 1940s conditions had improved and children again completed high school, although they had to attend the Elliston Centre school to do so.

Prior to 1943 children were not compelled by law to attend school. School attendance fluctuated considerably from day to day and from year to year. The length of time a child spent in the classroom depended partly on her own desire for an education, partly on her parents' attitude towards learning, and partly on family circumstances. Many a child anxious to go to school was prevented from doing so because he or she was needed at home. Earlier in the chapter I mentioned a girl who had to leave school with just Grade Two and assume the responsibility of running a home. Another, who entered service at age eleven, nevertheless got as far as Grade Four. A widow with six or seven young children could not keep them all in school. The youngest might attend, but the older ones would have to work to help support the family. Even if both parents were living, extreme poverty following a poor fishing season might keep children from school. And there were a few people who considered schooling

56

unnecessary, especially for one destined to be a fisherman or a fisherman's wife. "A scattered one (boy or girl) didn't go and parents with no education themselves did not force their children," said Aunt Hilda. Of course, stupid or slow learning children soon became school "drop-outs" because under the system still in force in the 1940s, all pupils were expected to know their lessons every day or be punished.

Girls' schooling was certainly not neglected. The majority of children who attended school were in the seven to twelve-year age bracket, and it is interesting to note that the girls attending school generally outnumbered the boys. Early records and local tradition alike indicate that most girls had as much opportunity as boys to obtain whatever education was available. It was customary even for those girls who entered service at ages twelve or thirteen to attend school from November 1 to April 30. They were usually in service for the six-month period between May 1 and October 31. Those who went to school full-time might put in two hundred days between September and June and most girls by the time they were thirteen or fourteen had reached the Grade Five Reader. At that point they dropped out of school unless they were academically inclined and meant to complete the High School grades. There was no general feeling that girls should not attend school. In fact, Aunt Hilda said, "Girls in some families went for something to do. They never learned very much."

Before 1920, those who had the ability and whose parents could afford it, after completing the courses offered in Elliston often went on to one of the St. John's high schools or to Normal School in St. John's. Perhaps this attitude toward higher education for girls was in some measure due to the fact that there had been a woman teacher in Maberly from the 1890s and through the early 1900s. Furthermore, around 1910, the high school teacher in Elliston Centre was a highly-qualified woman for her day. Parents saw that if their daughters were smart enough to pass the required courses they could choose some other career than that of domestic servant. In fact some girls were the top scholars in their families. In my mother's family, she, the only girl, was the one who went farthest in school, attended Normal School and became a teacher; her brothers were school drop-outs. There were still some people, even in the 1940s, who might say: "What's the use of educating a girl, she'll only get married." Or, "What's a big maid (girl) like you goin' to school for?" Generally speaking these individuals were those who had had very little or no education themselves and whose own children were dropouts.

In the early days there seem to have been no upper or lower age limits for school attendance. Most children were at least four years old when they started school. One woman, Lily Pearce, youngest of a large family, went to school when she was a toddler of three. She found it lonely at home with all her brothers and sisters in school; she had no one to play with. If she were in school her mother knew that one of the older children could "look-out to her."

Children might start school at any time in the year. Promotion in the early grades seems to have been based not on formal examinations but on the teacher's knowledge of the pupil. One woman, Rhoda Pearce, recalled going home and telling her father: "I'm through me book" she had completed a particular grade. "No one was in a grade in those days," said Edward Chaulk. If asked the extent of his education, a fisherman in the sixty-plus age group will likely say: "I was in number three," or "I got to number three."

My informants remembered quite vividly using the Royal Readers in school. These British texts used in Primer (The Fat Cat) to Number Six were the only textbooks the children had in the first few grades. People recalled that the difficult words in the lesson were listed at the beginning and there were pages of "useful knowledge."

The Readers strongly emphasize leading moral, upright and heroic lives. Many commented on the "sad" poems they had to learn. What they learned from their Readers in school really affected the students' lives. Years later they could recite entire poems they had memorized in school and some material even entered everyday talk. I have been told that one woman in Elliston always used to say on a stormy winter day: "It's as bad as the time Lucy Gray was lost!" referring to Wordsworth's poem which she had learned in Number Three.

The stress in school was on the three R's and memorization. Arithmetic was taught from separate texts from Grade One, but history and geography, as separate texts, were introduced around Grades Three and Four. For their geography, students even had to be able to "draw maps by heart."

Needlework for girls was a subject for examination in the early 1900s and also in the 1920s. There was a big, expensive textbook for this subject, but perhaps the teacher herself was the only one with a copy. Little time in school seems to have been devoted to this particular subject. Perhaps they were shown the different basic stitches and were urged to practice at home. Aunt Hilda mentioned that the examination consisted of making a certain item of clothing from special paper provided. Girls had to carry their own thread, scissors, and needle to the examination room. There was no needlework included in the curriculum of the 1940s, but I remember that one year we did practice some sewing after school hours. None of us was very interested because we were expected to make ourselves flannelette bloomers!

Religion was a subject for examination in the higher grades in New-foundland as late as the 1920s, but it does not seem to have been taught as a school subject in Elliston. Presumably Sunday School attendance and Church-going prepared a child for this.

Physical drill was also considered important in the early 1900s. Aunt Hilda said:

> Our school inspector left some books on health (hygiene) and after that we were oh, so particular about brushing our teeth and ex-cercising. Girls didn't wear slacks then and as the teacher was a man (Clarence Tilley) he wouldn't let the girls perform some of the exer-cises because they involved putting up their legs. About twenty min-utes a day was to be devoted to this physical drill.

By the 1940s, physical drill was not taught by the teacher. Apparently it was felt that the exercise a child got in those days, the running and jump-ing and fighting he or she did outside school, was sufficient.

Children in Elliston were fortunate in that in the late 1800s and early 1900s they were taught by fairly well-qualified teachers. In the Thirties also, Elliston children could study Grade Nine under a competent teacher when children of nearby Bonavista (population three or four times as great) did not have a suitably qualified teacher.

Students first sat for external examinations, when they did Primary, the first of the higher grades. These examinations, first introduced in 1895, were sent out from the Council of Higher Education in St. John's. In the early years the examinations were set and graded in Britain. Students re-ceived their results in late summer. Students were still writing C.H.E.'s in the 1940s. By then papers were being graded in St. John's but results were never released until late summer. Public examination results were always eagerly waited by the whole community even by those who had no chil-dren in school. The pupil who happened to come first in a particular grade was warmly congratulated and regarded as a celebrity, for a few days at least. To fail a grade was considered a terrible disgrace, but happily very few of those who wrote the public examinations had to face this experience in Elliston in the period prior to 1950. Potential failures had been weeded out already in the "survival of the fittest" system of education.

All of my older informants who were born in the Maberly-Neck section of Elliston went to school to "Aunt Annie" (Annie (Tilley) Pearce), "The Missus." Strong-willed and outspoken, she regulated her school as she saw fit. All the pupils put in five hours a day in the classroom with a late morning recess break of half an hour. During this break the teacher might visit a friend's home, such as my Grandmother Chaulk's. If she had a "cup of tea," by the time she got back to the school it would be time to dismiss the children for dinner. When I was a youngster, the school day began at 9:30 a.m. and continued until 12:30 p.m. with a fifteen minute recess break at 11:00 a.m. Afternoon sessions began at 2:00 p.m. and ended at 4:00 p.m.

Often, if otherwise engaged, "Aunt Annie" might employ some of her more advanced students to hear the lessons of the younger children. This system should have worked to the advantage of both, but some of those who were "taught" by such "student" teachers, reported that often their lessons would not be heard at all; instead they would be told all manner of nonsense and "blaggart," not stuff from the book. Not quite the sort of thing the school mistress would have sanctioned.

"Aunt Annie was a good reader, and if she read a particularly difficult passage, she would stop and explain it. On every Friday afternoon in the school year, she would read a short story or a chapter or two from some book. The pupils were expected to listen to this attentively and then reproduce it in writing word for word from memory. As a result, they were able to recount the stories orally to others outside the school and more people got pleasure from those stories than just those who listened in school.

My informants could not remember receiving marks from "Aunt Annie" for their school work. "It was a nip on the head if it was not done right or a word of praise if it was done well," said my Aunt Hilda. A "caning" was the usual punishment for misbehaviour and for failing to know lessons. Said Edward Chaulk: "The 'Missus' had a big long stick. She would give it to you anywhere with the stick, saying as she did so, 'Take that, me dear!' " I will mention later the repercussions at home when a child was punished in school.

The people who attended school during the early years of the century and even later, did most of their written work on slates using a "slate pencil". Girls might carry a rag and a small bottle of water to clean their

60

slates, but boys generally disdained this procedure, preferring to spit on their slates and wipe them clean with a sleeve. The only paper which pupils wrote on was in their "copybooks." These were used after they had learned their ABC's. "The pages were lined, with two 'copies,' usually proverbs per page," said Aunt Hilda. These copies were in "copper plate" handwriting and the pupils were expected to follow these examples as best they could. Most pupils found such writing hard to do, but there are several older people in Elliston today, among them Arthur (Tump) Tilley, whose writing is as "copper plate" and ornate as anything in the old copybooks. I have saved several envelopes from his Christmas cards because the writing was so elaborate.

Lessons in reading, spelling, history, geography, etc., were taken orally in the early 1900s. For answering questions the children usually stood in a row before the teacher's desk. By the 1940s the slates had been replaced by "scribblers" and "exercise books." (lined writing pads), and lead pencils. Yet the "standing up" in class still persisted in elementary grades. Teachers moved pupils "up head and down last" according to their ability to spell or answer questions orally. In spelling class if a child spelt a word incorrectly it was passed along the row until someone knew it. If that someone was not already head of the class he would move up the line past all who could not spell the word. "Spelling Bees" or contests were unknown in the early days in Elliston schools and they were held only occasionally in the 1940s. Position in class could be an ever changing thing. In some classes there was keen rivalry for the top spot; in others, none at all. It depended on the individuals in the classes.

All of the schools in the Elliston area, except for those built in the late Fifties and Sixties, were heated by coal and wood-burning pot-bellied Dixies. During the wintertime the bigger boys took turns lighting the morning fire. In the days when wood was the chief fuel, each child was expected to bring along a "junk" (piece of wood perhaps 20″ long and 6″ in diameter) for the fire each day. Speaking of her first day at school, Lily Pearce said: "With a junk of wood under my arm I went over to the school door and knocked." During the coal-burning era of the Forties, children were expected to supply the "splits," smaller pieces of wood for kindling the coal fire, the fuel being now supplied by the school board. Older girls were responsible for sweeping and dusting the classroom every Friday afternoon after school. I don't remember if this included cleaning the lamp chimneys, because these were fragile, but I know we were assigned in pairs. When two "buddies" worked together it became play-work. Periodically the schools might be closed early or for all Friday afternoon for "scrubbing." Then all the mothers, or older sisters or older girl pupils were expected to turn up at the school each with a pail of water, soap, and a scrubbing brush, to give the place a thorough cleaning. The odour of "Jeye's Fluid" permeated the air, for this disinfectant was always added to the cleaning water.

In the early 1900s pupils worked at long wooden slanting desks with iron legs which might or might not be fastened to the floor. A bench having no back rest was attached and the whole could seat three or four pupils. By the 1940s there were separate wooden desks (tables) and folding wooden chairs. But some "old desks" were still in use in Maberly school in the 1940s for temporary seating when the registration was higher than anticipated.

Discipline was strict in the early schools and also during the Forties. But that did not silence some rebellious natures. There was usually one pupil who just could not agree with the teacher and who would not submit to classroom discipline. His school career was usually brief. And there were times when the teacher had to admit to being mistaken. On one such occasion in an early teacher's career she kept the school "after school" because of one person's wrongdoing. A rebellious girl, not willing to be punished unjustly, jumped to her feet and ran to the door, and turning to the others shouted: "Come on, ya buggers!" They followed her and there was no later punishment for this unheard-of action. But generally there was little to disrupt the school day. The teacher expected obedience in school no matter how difficult the assignment. Besides if a child was punished in school for anything, he rarely got any sympathy at home. Quite the opposite!

Most of the people I talked to reported that boys were often "given a lacing," that is, whipped with a razor strop, or belt or rope. Girls rarely, if ever, received this punishment. The most bestowed on a girl was an occasional maternal slap. Many parents in the early days used fear of persons outside the immediate family as a means of control. There were no policemen or any other authoritative uniformed men who lived in the community, so the person chosen was usually a bearded man who lived some distance from the child's home. Orpah Crewe, who grew up on the Point, admitted that as a child she was frightened of a bearded man who lived in Sandy Cove. Even after she was married she said she still kept a trace of her childhood fear of that particular individual.

# Chapter 4
## The Young Woman:
## Courtship and Marriage

By the time a girl was a teenager she had been thoroughly indoctrinated in the accepted ways of doing things and the code of behaviour. If she stayed at home she assumed a greater share of the family work load, taking more responsibility for the younger children and running the home. In spite of her workload she became more involved in social activities and relationships with the young men of the community.

For the teenage girl, then as now, clothing was a matter of great importance. All those I talked to about fashions in the early 1900s stressed the strong emphasis on modesty. Teenagers then dressed much like their mothers, skirts were the same length and both had the same number of layers of clothing. It was considered essential that the body be completely covered.

How thoroughly this was followed can best be seen from the masculine point of view. Speaking of the years before 1920, Aubrey Pearce summed up the boys' attitude to the girls' fashions of his youth thus:

"See a naked leg then you'd go crazy. Everything covered up. You were wondering . . . ."

Mothers usually instilled the need for modesty in their daughters when the latter were very young. On washday, women's underclothing, even that of little girls, had to be dried "away from the men's eyes,"[1] said Aunt Hilda. This prudery continued until well into the 1920s and to this day is still expressed by some of the older generation. As for the layers of clothing they wore, my Aunt Hilda who was a teenager during the early 1900s, had this to say in a letter:

> The young and old seemed to dress alike. By that I mean as soon as a girl started to develop she wore the same as her older sisters or even her mother in those years.
>
> At the age of twelve or thirteen we wore corsets with bones all around, they came up to the armpits. Was formed to do the same as a bra does now. They came over the hips but not too far, not as long as the corsets of today. We hated to wear them but it was said to strengthen the back. I don't think so. We still wore our two petticoats but it was a corset cover, for the top, then. We always wore pinafores or bib aprons.

For dirty work outside or inside the house women and girls wore rough aprons of "brin," (burlap), or of "burney cotton" (cotton material sold cheaply by the pound because it has become discoloured or soiled).

Blouses and skirts were worn sometimes by women. The skirts were made of the same material [fine serge or a woolen cloth] as were the dresses. The skirts or bottoms of dresses would be flat at the front waist but quite full at the back. The waist would be tight fitting with tucks and frills up the front, a lot of work would have gone into it as the tucks would be so small and the stitches also. The sleeves would be puffed at the shoulders but tight fitting at the wrist. The collars would be high and in order to keep them from wrinkling a bone on each side would be attached which would reach to the ears. Sometimes the skirts would be trimmed with braid, at least those of heavier material. Since the skirts were quite long and the roads often either muddy or dusty, each woman would have to use one hand to lift her skirts from gathering a lot of dirt. Summer dresses, which were made of lighter materials called "winsey", had quite a number of ruffles; looked very pretty. The coats would be tight fitting with a gathering at the back.

Hats worn at the time were very large with a place on the underside to fit over the bun. Hatpins about a foot long would fasten the hat to the hair. The heads of those pins were large and of different colours. The pins were also used by the young ladies as a protective measure against improper advances. When a lady went visiting or to church, gloves were a *must*. In summer these were in a white cotton fabric, but at other times of the year they were of black kid. Black and white were the only colours worn. The high shoes [boots] that were worn were laced and later buttoned. It seems that the same footwear was worn winter and summer as the boots were sturdy, or maybe the winter boots would be of leather and the summer ones of kid, as there were no overshoes at the time. Stockings were black knitted ones.

In the early 1900s, older girls who had finished school wore their hair long, just as the younger school girls did, but, like their mothers, they often pulled it into a bun on the top, or at the back of the head.

Through the 1920s and '30s teenage girls' lives — their work, their pleasures, and their pastimes — remained essentially what it had been earlier in the century. But styles in girls' clothing were gradually changing through the 1920s, even in Elliston, responding to the general outside trend. By the thirties and forties, teenage girls' styles were quite different from those of sedate older women. Skirts were now up to the knee; corsets were unheard of, except for stout matrons; low shoes had replaced high button boots; and most dresses and skirts varied in style and materials, coming mainly ready-made from the stores in Elliston and Bonavista. Most girls and younger women cut their hair short in the "boy's bob" or had it tightly "permed," i.e., permanently waved, at a beauty parlor in Bonavista, before "home perms" were widely used. Hats were still worn in church but otherwise, in fine summer weather, most women and girls went bareheaded. Some, more careful of their complexions than others, wore a "slouch," a sunbonnet, to protect them from sunburn as they worked on the flake or in the garden. In recent years bandanas have been the standard head covering for girls and women during inclement weather. Prior to bandanas, older women wore "the cloud" (a heavy square scarf).

Although most parents were especially strict with their daughters over the way of dressing and their behaviour with boys, mothers gave very little advice or information to their growing daughters about sex. One woman, Jane Pearce said: "[we were] never told nothin!" They did not discuss "growing up" with them and menstruation would never be mentioned in the presence of menfolk. On no account must the boys of the family be aware that a girl was having "those" days, and before the 1940s they were difficult enough times, for girls had none of today's many products to serve their needs. Most young girls got their information from other girls, often an older sister. In the 1900s they were further hampered by the fact that there was little or no literature on the subject available to them. The information they picked up came through their friends who somehow were better informed about such "dirty" matters, from over-hearing older women talking about such things, and perhaps by asking a helpful married sister or older friend. This was one subject on which I got very little information, for most older women were still hesitant about discussing such topics even though I was a married woman.

Generally, girls were supposed to be kept "innocent" and inquisitiveness about sex was almost considered a sin. No parent wanted a daughter "to get herself in trouble" though how they expected them to understand such matters is unclear. In the early days, as now, some children were born out of wedlock. Usually though, if a girl became pregnant, marriage followed soon after. Of course there were a few girls in the 1940s and I suspect, in the early 1900s, who were considered fair game by adolescent boys. They were as willing as the boys to participate in sexual play.

During the period before 1920 "good" girls were expected to be home at a "decent" hour, by ten o'clock. They did not "beat the roads" till "all hours of the night." Walking "on the road" — in Elliston, on the stretch of road between the Churches and Mark's Path on the Bonavista Road — was the usual pastime for young unmarried adults. In summer such evening walks might depend on there being no fish "to put away." If there were, a girl might have to work in the stage, or if she were "in service," might have to "mind the house" while her mistress worked "down below." But Sunday after church service, winter or summer, was the accepted time for going for a stroll or "over on the road," unless the weather was too disagreeable.

Even while strolling with no adults nearby, young ladies were expected to behave properly. Usually groups of girls would stroll along, followed or preceded by groups of boys. Often the boys would be seated along the roadside by clumps of rocks. Banter would be exchanged between the different groups as some girls did not mind talking back and forth or "carrying on." Although boys were permitted to sing on the road, well brought-up girls of the early 1900s were not supposed to do so, nor were they to talk or laugh loudly. To do so was considered vulgar and coarse. This same notion persisted in the 1940s. Even then "a girl who thought anything of herself" behaved as correctly as did the young ladies a generation or two earlier. After a certain period of parading back and forth, groups dispersed. Some younger teenage girls and boys, of course, went home as they came, in groups of three and four. Couples went their separate ways. Other shyer sweethearts would leave the "road" separately, but the girl would not be far on her homeward way before she met 'not merely by chance,' her fellow, or one who hoped to become her fellow. One cannot help wondering whether the short road named "Trick'em" which is a short cut to the Maberly-Neck road, might not have taken its name from this practice among shy lovers.

This Sunday walking was often the only chance most older boys and girls had of being together. There were no places to "hang out," for the stores of the community were mostly general stores run by older men and were usually the gathering place for adult males only. Not until the 1940s was there a "restaurant," i.e., a "juke-box joint" with soft drinks and candy — no meals were served there — and it was about this time also that movies were shown occasionally in the Orange Hall.

In the early 1900s there were no public dances in Elliston though dancing was practised all through the year by a few, mostly Anglican young people, who danced in their own homes. Aunt Hilda used to reminisce sometimes about the dancing that took place in her home in Maberly. She said friends of theirs, some of them Methodists, used to come from as far away as the North Side to enjoy the fun. She didn't say if her friends' parents knew about the dancing or if they were strongly against dancing themselves. But dancing and card-playing were two pastimes frowned upon by strict Methodists and Salvationists. By the late 1920s attitudes seem to have changed slightly. Then a favourite gathering spot for dancing during the summertime was on the bridge at Sandy Cove. Here, to the music of accordion and mouth organ (harmonica) young people could dance away and bother no one, since the nearest house was more than a half mile away. Dancing, however, was not permitted in the school, hall, or in most homes even in the 1940s.

Of course there were "times and concerts" (described in a later chapter) in the Orange Hall and in the different schools of the community, but these were usually held around Christmas time only. There was little public entertainment at any other time of the year. In the early years, however, in May or early June and again in August, picnics were held by the different Sunday Schools. At the picnics everything was free.

During the late 1930s and until the 1950s, garden parties, sponsored by the different religious denominations, were held in Elliston and nearby communities during August. People of all ages patronized their own local

67

affairs and, in addition, the younger people usually went to those in the nearby places. This gave boys and girls an opportunity to meet on a "week night." Similarly, during Christmas, times and concerts would be attended by boys from neighbouring places. Aside from visiting relatives for a week or so, these events were the only ways boys and girls could meet young people outside their own community.

The chief entertainment for the older boys and girls at these affairs was the "rings," the closest most of them came to dancing. Younger children played "rings" too, but the marriageable young people were the main participants. Ring games, whether they included singing or not, were acceptable to the Methodists, as there was no "music," i.e., instrumental music. Two "rings" my informants remembered playing were "King William was King George's Son" and "Jolly Miller", and a popular "ring game" was "Catch the Third."

For "King William," all those taking part joined hands, forming a circle around one person, either a boy or a girl. Then, singing the following verses, they danced around him or her:

> King William was King George's son,
> And all the royal race he won,
> And on his breast a star he wore,
> Point me to the Governor's door.
>
> Come choose to the East,
> Come choose to the West,
> Choose the very one that you love best.
> If she's [he's] not there to take your part,
> Choose another one with all your heart.
>
> Down on this carpet you must kneel,
> As the grass grows in the field.
> Kiss your partner, kiss her sweet,
> You may rise upon your feet.

At the words "Come choose to the East" etc. the person in the centre of the ring chose a girl or a boy as her [his] partner. Kneeling in the centre of the ring, they kissed. Then the person that had been brought into the ring chose another for his partner, and so the game continued, until most had had a turn in the centre of the ring.[2]

For "Jolly Miller," there was an uneven number of players. All the participants, except one, formed couples, arm in arm, one behind the other, forming a double ring, with the odd one in the centre. As they sang the following verse, they moved around the person in the centre:

> There was a jolly miller and he lived by himself,
> By grinding corn he made his wealth.
> One hand in his pocket, the other in the bag,
> The wheel went round and he made his grab.

At the word "grab," they let go arms and grabbed for another partner. The player in the centre (the miller) tried to secure a partner and a place while they were changing places. If he managed to do this, the odd person became miller in his stead.[3]

"Catch the Third" was a popular game, especially with young adults. It required an odd number of players. They formed themselves in pairs in a ring, one pair behind the other. In one place there were three in a row, the one standing on the inner side towards the centre being the "Third." This was a running game, for the "Third" had to leave his place and be chased by another member of the group, usually a person he himself chose, one he liked especially. If he eluded capture and got back in his place, he might be chased again by someone else. If caught, he had to take his place with those who remained standing still while the "catching" was going on.

Of course boys and girls of marriageable age had to put up with a lot of joking and teasing in some houses and heard all sorts of sayings and superstitions concerning love and marriage. Both were warned about taking the last piece of bread or cake on the plate. If they did so it meant spinsterhood or bachelorhood.[4] A girl who sat on the table "wanted a man."[5] And falling upstairs meant a wedding in the family within twelve months.[6]

Girls and boys, in the early days, as now, varied in the amount of interest they showed in the opposite sex. Some girls were known "to be breakin' their necks for a man" while others were less obvious. A girl had various ways of finding out if a certain boy liked her. Two burning matches might be named for the girl and the one she liked. If the "boy" bent toward the "girl" then he cared for her. Another method a girl might use was to take a burning match and hold it between her thumb and forefinger till it burnt itself out. If in burning the match bent over toward her hand it meant the boy was "burning" with love for her.[7]

These rites, which could be practiced at any time of the year, were done mainly for entertainment by the "sillier" girls and were not taken very seriously. Those divination rites which were carried out on Midsummer Day, June 24th, however, were believed by most girls to have special significance, and it is my impression these were practiced only when a girl became seriously interested in boys and wished to find out about her matrimonial prospects. Quite a number of different rites were performed. Most of them had to be begun on Midsummer Eve and events were noted until noon on Midsummer Day. Elderly fishermen might take note of the weather that day and so diagnose the weather for the rest of the summer, but young girls were interested in more than just the summer weather.

These Midsummer Day divination rites went under the general title of "trying your man" or "tryin' your fellow." For the most important one, a girl put the white of an egg in a glass of water on Midsummer Eve. She then placed the glass on a window sill to catch the first rays of the morning sun on June 24th. The egg white was supposed "to rise with the sun." Just before noon the girl would examine the forms within the glass to see if there might be any clue to her future husband's work. Quite frequently a girl saw the sails of a full-rigged ship, especially if the fellow she especially fancied was a fisherman, as he was ninety-nine percent of the time! Thus her future mate would be connected with the sea and boats. Having studied the forms in the glass, she then took the mixture and threw it on the main roadway at twelve noon and stationed herself to see what man first stepped over it. The initials, or at least the initial of the surname of the future husband would be the same as his.[8] One woman, Nina Pearce, remembered that on one Midsummer Day she was very annoyed when she saw a widower, twice married, step over the egg which she had thrown in the main pathway. However, not just the initial but his surname (Pearce) was the same as that of the man she later married. Another woman, Mary Jane Porter, now in her sixties, said that the first person to step over her egg on one June 24th became her husband a few years later though they had not been "keeping company" at the time he stepped over the egg.

There were other divination rites practiced on Midsummer's Day. One traditional way of finding out about one's future mate was to put a silk handkerchief on the grass overnight. The dew was supposed to form the initial of one's sweetheart.[9] Since few girls were in a position to afford a silk handkerchief, it was probably not a common practice.

In Elliston, another method was to put a "snail", i.e. slug, in an envelope and seal the envelope. The snail's crawling or moving about inside

70

the envelope was supposed to trace out the future mate's initials.[10] I have no further explanation on how this was done.

One very common rite was this: A girl cut the letters of the alphabet out of paper and turned them face down in a saucepan or some other container. She then sprinkled in a little sand and some water. The letters that turned up overnight were supposed to be the initials of her future sweetheart. One informant now in her forties tried this experiment when she was a young teenager and was quite annoyed when two letters came up that did not suit any of the local boys that she liked. But the man that she married a few years later had the same initials as those that came up in the sand.[11]

Mary Jane Porter gave another method for finding out about one's sweetheart. The girl had to go outdoors at precisely midnight on Midsummer's Eve and scatter oat seeds, saying as she did:

Oat seed I set, Oat seed I sow,
Whoever is my sweetheart,
Come after me and mow.

Since most women were extremely fearful of going outdoors alone in the dark even in the 1940s, it is doubtful that this rite was performed very often. This practice was widely known in England, but hemp seed, not oat seed, was mentioned.[12]

So important was Midsummer Day to young girls at or near marriageable age in Elliston in the early part of the century that it was called "Sweetheart's Day." On no other special day were similar rites performed. Girls still observed the old customs during the 1940s, but I don't think many girls do so nowadays.

### COURTSHIP

Courtships varied according to the individuals involved. Some girls had lots of boy friends before getting serious; others married their first and only boy friend. Some couples "kept company" for such a short period of time before their marriage that someone would be sure to remark. "It must have been a case of 'ask and have'." The courting days of others were so long drawn out that the couple seemed like a permanent fixture "on the road." In the summertime and even during the winter most courting couples would parade up and down the main road during the early part of the evening. Then they might return to his or her home, or settle down in some sheltered nook for more serious courting.

In the early days and especially in the thirties and forties courting couples were apt to be "dogged" by younger people, usually young boys, who would attempt to spy on their activities. Sometimes couples were unaware of such scrutiny, and at other times the boys simply tagged along a few feet behind, teasing and tormenting the courting couple and giving them no privacy. Mr. Edwin Baker, during one of my conversations with him, related with glee how he and another boy "dogged" a young man who was courting the minister's servant girl. Apparently he was a bit of a "dandy" and wore a light coloured suit on Sundays. He and his girl used to spend a lot of time seated on a huge rock that used to be by the side of the road in Sandy Cove. One night the boys went there before them and sprinkled particles of "razum pitch" on the surface of the rock. Most of this came off and stuck to the young man's trousers, spoiling them.

The neighbouring communities had the same custom of walking back and forth on the road, and it was usual on Sundays for boys from Elliston to walk to Bonavista, five miles away, to try their luck with the girls there and for Bonavista boys to come "over the Ridge" "after" Elliston girls. When bicycles became common, Catalina or Little Catalina, both approximately ten miles away, might be the place for the Elliston boys' Sunday jaunts. Even by the 1950s cars had little effect on the courting pattern for there were just a few of them around and most of these were driven by older married men.

Parents probably felt this mingling with young people from outside the community was a good thing though they did not openly encourage it. Many families in Elliston are related, and "close relatives are not supposed to marry." Some parents strengthened this statement by pointing out that sometimes children born of first-cousin marriages were "feeble-minded" and would cite one or two examples in the community. It was believed that children of such unions would be unlucky in life, sickly, and generally things would not go right for them. Such beliefs had their effect, for a fair number of girls married outside the community. Despite these strictures the majority of girls did marry local boys, so marriage between second cousins was not uncommon. Boys who sought their brides outside Elliston brought new women into the community.

When couples who were "going together" decided to get married, they might inform their families and start preparing for the wedding, but there was no formal engagement. No ring was given until the wedding band was placed on the bride's finger. Sarah Chaulk, however, said she had a "sort of engagement ring." She wore "a heart and a half" ring which her "fellow" gave her before their marriage. Another woman, married in the 1940s, said: "No engagement ring. I didn't get mine till long after I was married."

It seems the majority of girls in Elliston in the early 1900s were married before they reached their mid-twenties. Many of my informants were married between the ages of seventeen and twenty. There was no "proper age" for marriage; it depended on the individuals involved. Aunt Hilda when asked if people got married younger in the old days than at present, replied:

> Well, it was the same then as it is now. Not many reached the age of twenty-three or twenty-four. Some were married at eighteen. On the whole perhaps it was in their early twenties they were married. It depended on the circumstances. I think it was just the same then as now. I see changes. There's quite a change for each generation says "I don't know what this new generation is coming to!" I don't find one generation any worse than another.

Weddings were more informal than they are nowadays. There was no attempt to have the wedding party dressed in any uniform fashion; all wore their best, the men their Sunday suits, and the girls their best dresses. Usually the bride tried to have an especially nice new dress, plus other accessories, and the groom invested in a new blue serge suit. The bride didn't worry about a "going away" outfit for there was no honeymoon.

Some of the brides in the early 1900s wore veils, but frequently they wore white hats instead. And in very early days, it seems the brides wore special "wedding bonnets." One which was worn by my great-grandmother Tilley, a bride in the 1850s, is of straw with fancy embroidery around the crown. It is very small and must have just "perched" on the crown of her head. Brides in the early 1900s usually wore white gloves, white stockings and white shoes even for a winter wedding, so they must have had some sort of feeling that it was right to have white at a wedding, even though the wedding dress was usually not white.

Dresses were street length and until the forties, of course, this meant

73

mid-calf, or even ankle-length. The material chosen for the dress depended on the bride's circumstances. Sometimes it would be made at home, but more often than not such an important dress would be "store-bought." It would be bought off the rack, perhaps in one of the Bonavista stores which had a wider selection of clothing than did the Elliston ones. If the bride-to-be were better-off than average, she might send to one of the St. John's department stores for a suitable dress and accessories. A soft crepe material seems to have been the choice of most women for this important dress. However, one woman, Emily (Pearce) Tilley, wore white lace over robin's egg blue satin for her wedding in 1914. Her veil was shoulder length with a wreath of flowers on the forehead. This veil was a gift from the groom's brother who bought it in St. John's.

My mother, a bride of the late 1920s, wore a mid-calf length, apricot-coloured crepe dress with long sleeves. Her veil was shoulder length and was attached to a circlet of wax orange blossoms. She wore a string of beads which exactly matched her dress.

The so-called "traditional" long white bridal gown was not traditional in Elliston in the early years, nor in the 1940s. Most brides favoured blue. "Married in blue, always be true" was the saying. Although most girls knew the rhyme:

Married in white, you have chosen all right.
Married in grey, you will live far away.
Married in black, you will wish yourself back.
Married in red, you will wish yourself dead.
Married in green, ashamed to be seen.
Married in blue, he will always be true.
Married in pearl, you will live in a whirl.
Married in yellow, ashamed of your fellow.
Married in brown, you will live out of town.
Married in pink, your spirits will sink.[13]

One informant mentioned someone she knew who had been married in yellow. She remarked: "She was ashamed of him all right. She only lived with him for six months or so and then she left him."
Generally a girl chose a dress that would serve her for "best" for a few years after the wedding.

The bridal bouquet of natural flowers has become fashionable in Elliston only in recent years, for there were few flower gardens and no "nurseries" nearby. Besides, weddings were rarely held in the summertime as this was the season for work. They might take place at any other season of the year and then natural flowers were unavailable. So if a bride carried a bouquet, it was of artificial crepe-paper flowers made by some woman in the community. The men in the wedding party wore paper roses in their lapels. Often instead of a bouquet, the bride carried a prayer book decorated with ribbons.

The wedding ceremony was never rehearsed beforehand. The titles "maid of honour" and "best man" were not in use. The chief attendants were the "father-giver" and the "mother-giver," and the other attendants, if there were any others, were dubbed "bridesgirls" and "bridesboys." The father-giver was a cross between the "father" and the best man; he performed both duties. On the one hand, when the minister asked "who giveth this woman" he responded, but he still stayed in this position and "supported" the groom. However he did not carry the ring; the groom himself had this. The mother-giver had the same responsibilities as today's maid of honour.

Although people were poor, the wedding ring was never handmade as seems to have been the custom in some parts of the United States; the husband always managed to have a gold ring for his bride's finger. This plain wide band, costing $10 or so, was in later years probably bought in Elliston or Bonavista, but in earlier days had to be bought in St. John's.[14] It was often the incorrect size, but if it were a bit big, the wife might wear some cheaper ring as a guard to keep it from slipping off. Since no woman would think of taking her ring off at any time, it was not uncommon to see a woman wearing her wedding ring on the middle finger of her left hand when she was washing clothes or washing fish. I remember my mother wearing hers on her middle finger.

When both bride and groom came from the same section of the community, they walked to the wedding — bride, groom, attendants and the congregation. For instance, if one or both of them were Anglican in Maberly (Muddy Brook), the marriage ceremony would probably take place in the Anglican school-chapel on the "Schoolhouse Hill." One couple, Jane and Aubrey Pearce, married some fifty years or more, recalled that for their wedding in December it snowed a bit, "just nice for walking." Usually if either the bride or groom were Anglican and one came from Elliston Centre while the other came from Maberly, the wedding ceremony would be performed in the little Anglican church located at Elliston Centre. If the wedding reception were being held in "The Cove," the bridal party usually walked. If the reception were being held in Maberly the couple and their attendants would ride in horse and carriage (buggy) in spring, summer, and fall, but on horse and riding sleigh in the winter time.

A couple married in the Anglican church could not have a surprise wedding for their banns had to be published for three Sundays previous to their marriage. Neither could they be married in Lent. If for some reason they wanted to marry during that time they had to ask a United Church minister or a Salvation Army officer to perform the ceremony.

Couples who were married by the United Church or Salvation Army did not necessarily have a "church" wedding. Sometimes the marriage took place in the church parsonage or in a private home. The number of people who attended the religious ceremony had little bearing on the number who attended the reception later. Most marriage ceremonies were performed in the late afternoon or early evening: three and four p.m. were hours mentioned for afternoon weddings, while seven p.m. seems to have been a popular time for evening weddings. People knew the rhyme:

Monday for health
Tuesday for wealth
Wednesday's the best of all
Thursday for losses
Friday for crosses
And Saturday no day at all![15]

Few considered any day unlucky for a wedding, though one woman had her reservations about Friday.[16]

It was customary for men to "fire off" guns along the route taken by the wedding party after the ceremony.

No informants could recall any runaway marriages, but there were cases of quick or surprise marriages. These people slipped off to Bonavista or Catalina and were married there with no fanfare at all. But such cases were few and were a favourite topic of gossip for months afterward. There was also considerable gossip if there was a great disparity in age between husband and wife. Usually such marriages were between older widowers and young girls, rather than between an old bachelor and a young girl, and although people gossiped they recognized the necessity of the man's marrying. In a fishing community a fisherman had to have a woman to take part in the operation, if he were partners with someone and not just an ordinary shareman. If his mother or a sister could not perform the nec-

76

essary work in the stage or on the flake, he had to look around for a suitable helpmate — one who could pull her weight. A man who was skipper certainly was expected to have female help as he very probably got the lion's share of the "voyage" (proceeds from the sale of cod).

Up until the 1940s, a wedding was thought of as a community social occasion. Invitations were given orally by family members, and people would sometimes come to the reception even if they had somehow been overlooked when people were being asked to the wedding.

Everyone liked to contribute in some way, especially if the couple were well-liked in the community. Cakes, pies, and pastries, all manner of sweet delicacies, would be brought or sent to the reception by the women of the community. Often the dish on which a cake was brought to the wedding was the wedding gift. Wedding gifts were ordinarily brought to the reception instead of being sent to the bride in advance as is the custom nowadays. An area was set aside for the display of the wedding gifts, and guests might see what the young couple had received.

There was no set rule as to where the reception would be held. Sometimes it was held at the home of the bride's parents, sometimes at the groom's parents, and not infrequently in the new home of the bridal pair. Until the 1940s all receptions were held in private homes. Guests crowded into every room in the house and took up all available space. There was not much room for many kinds of games, but there was a lot of talking, joking, and "carrying-on." If the bride and groom were to sleep in the house where the reception was being held, some guests would be sure to play a few tricks on them. The favourite was fixing the bed so that it would collapse when the pair got into it.

The reception would carry on late into the night, and often a wedding reception was a two-night affair. Those who could not make it the first night tried to get there on the second. The second night guests were usually the older, more sedate members of the community and things would not be so boisterous as on the previous night. Perhaps because of the temperance movement, which was strong in the community during the first decades of the century, no liquor was served at weddings.

There was always a special "wedding cake." This was usually a rich fruit cake, very like the traditional Christmas cake. Everyone at the wedding had to have a piece of it. A young unmarried girl never ate her piece of wedding cake at the wedding. She wrapped it carefully and placed it under her pillow "to dream on" when she went to bed that night. Many believed that if a girl slept with a piece of wedding cake under her pillow she would dream of her future husband. This bit of folklore is widespread and was a common practice in Dorsetshire and other English counties, as is noted by Udal in his *Dorsetshire Folk-Lore*[17] This is not surprising since the ancestors of many people in Elliston were from Dorset and other West Country counties.

Here is how Aunt Hilda described a wedding reception around 1910:

> They didn't send out invitations then. It was all after the bride and groom had their cup of tea. They went around to all the houses in the immediate vicinity and asked them to come. After the brides-maids and boys had their tea, they would leave them and go around. Just the bride and groom would go. Several weddings around that time were conducted in this fashion. They have more means now for doing things but even in those days everyone had a large reception. Everyone in the community was invited. No matter how poor you were. For they all brought a contribution to set the table.

The length of time the newlyweds had been "going together", and their ages, would determine what material effects they had to start married life with. Some brides who were older, or who had been courting for a long period, had chests full of the following items: bed clothes — sheets, quilts, pillow slips, pillows, etc.; tablecloths, often decorated with fancy stitching; dresser sets in knitted or crocheted lace; colourful hooked mats; cushions already stuffed with feathers, and so on. Others, barely eighteen years of age, perhaps just getting by on a servant girl's wages, would have less to contribute. A youthful husband would rarely have a home of his own to take his bride to, so the couple would live with relatives for a while at least. Here they would not need the items required for maintaining a separate household. They used what was already in the home and both fitted into the work team of the household as best they could.

Most young men, however, did not do serious courting until they felt they could afford to keep a wife as well as she had been accustomed to, for "sensible" girls looked for a "good provider" and he had to be able to make a living for a family. There was nothing in the way of government assistance to fall back on, and many in the earlier years, unlike today, were too proud to rely on such assistance. A man felt at a disadvantage, for example, if he was a fisherman and the girl he was courting was a teacher, for not only was she supporting herself on her salary, but also she was often helping out at home as well. He would have to be very sure that they could live comfortably on his earnings before he asked her to marry him. A man courting a "servant girl" in Elliston certainly did not have this obstacle in his way, for her wages were very low and she might have been in service since she was twelve years old. If she married young, she would be working just as hard or perhaps harder, but at least she could feel she was working for herself.

*Badger's Quay — woman scrubbing mats — early 1940's*

*Carmanville — woman milking goat — early 1940's*

*Maberly — "washing out" saltbulk fish — Mother, uncle and shareman — early 1950's*

*Badger's Quay — woman sawing wood — 1950's*

*Mother in her flower garden — early 1950's*

*"boil up", berry picking — 1950's*

*Rhonda Pearce with her spinning wheel — wheel in continual use until 1940's*

*washing out the wool — late 1950's*

*Aunt Bess Tilly "at the grass" — Her grandfather was William White of the* **Tickle Cove Pond** *song — 1920's*

*Ploughing the potato garden — 1920's method unchanged through the 1950's*

*Ray, Aunt Hilda, Father in the "Big Midder" — 1920's*

*Aunt Fanny, Mary Jane, Mother, Aunt Rebecca resting after spreading the grass — late 1920's*

*horse and carriage ride — 1920's*

*baby in pram late — 1920's*

*Roy Tucker's homemade car — 1940's — Roy, a polio victim, had his friends push the car up a hill and he rode it down. He later drove a taxi.*

*return of Arthur Chaulk from World War II —     one of Elliston's three cars*

*Grandfather Tilley's casket, covered in brocade of a color signifying his age — 1936*

*from left — Mary Jane Chaulk (Porter), Walter Chaulk, Fanny Chaulk (Porter), unidentified children — 1920's (Empire Day)*

*Fanny's and Mary Jane's children are shown here in their Sunday best. Mary Jane's two are in the centre and Fanny's on either end — 1930's*

*North side women and girls with their bake apples — 1930's*

*Aunt Hilda, Aunt Fanny, Father, Grandmother Chaulk, Uncle Sam — early 1920's*

*Maberly's first school, built in 1890's — also used for church services — Mother taught there until she married — 1920's*

*Elliston school — 1920's*

*Maberly — the flakes — 1950's*

*stageheads during the storm — men saving the longers — stageheads were soon after destroyed — fall 1950's*

*Noder Cove — northside Elliston 1930's*

*Maberly — view from the Head — 1950's*

*Elliston — view from Lodge Hill showing Salvation Army barracks, lower left,
United Church, centre, and school, right 1928*

*boats on the Collar, Elliston North — 1928*

# Chapter 5
## The Woman and Her Family:
## Pregnancy, Childbirth, and Infant Care

People would expect a woman to be "in the family way" within a year of marriage, since motherhood was considered a woman's central role. Large families were the rule; most women were more or less regularly occupied with problems of pregnancy, childbirth and infant care. This chapter will describe traditional language, practices, and beliefs; for example, the terms people used to describe a pregnant woman's condition depending on whether she were married or unmarried; the beliefs that prenatal influences might mark, retard, or cripple the unborn child; the treatment accorded the new mother; her special celebration with friends and neighbours some days after the birth; different christening practices; and the care of the baby: its food, medicines, clothing, and general comfort.

In the early 1900s, pregnancy was not discussed as freely as it is today. A married woman was said to be "in the family way" or "that way again, you know." Rarely, if ever, was the term "pregnant" used. A girl who became pregnant out of wedlock would be termed "knocked up" by the coarser element and said to have "got in trouble" by the majority. When a baby arrived fairly soon after a marriage, then everybody knew "she (the mother) had to be married." If the child arrived before the girl's marriage, such an illegitimate child might be referred to casually as "a merry-begot." Some neighbours would silence one inclined to be nasty or high-minded about the matter by saying: "Don't halloo till you're out of the woods. You have daughters of your own." Or, the commonest solace given the girl's parents was "She's not the first and she won't be the last." Generally speaking those who strayed were not discriminated against and might later marry successfully. Sometimes the child was reared by the mother's parents as their own offspring; other times he went to live with his mother and her husband, who might or might not be his father.

It was generally believed that the actions, desires, and conduct of an expectant mother affected her unborn baby. So she was expected to observe certain taboos connected with pregnancy, as well as to take care of herself physically. In the latter stages of pregnancy she was expected to be extremely careful of how she moved. She was warned against raising her arms too far above her head, for fear she might "cord" the baby.[1] Too much bending was not good for her either, but no specific consequences were attributed to this action.

One curious belief I encountered was this: a pregnant woman was not supposed to put anything to her nose to smell — a flower, for instance. The woman who told me this belief however used to do this very thing. She said she loved the perfume given off by "Sweet Rockets," a flower which grew in several gardens in the community. She would hold the flower to her nose and breathe deeply, and her child was not affected. Obviously she did not take this belief seriously and her conduct was not guided by it.

It was believed that "birthmarks" could come about for various reasons. If the mother were startled by some object's being tossed toward her and hitting her, or if she accidentally bumped herself, a "birthmark" might be expected to show up in the same place on the baby.[2] However, they were believed chiefly to be the result of some unsatisfied craving by the mother during her pregnancy.[3] At the very least, an unsatisfied "craving" might cause the child to be fretful until he received the food his mother did not get.[4]

It was taken for granted that all women had "cravings" for certain foods when they were in "that" condition. And young fathers-to-be often went to great lengths to satisfy expectant wives' wishes for certain foods. No one wanted a marked child. Also, people outside the immediate family were usually careful to see that an expectant woman's cravings were satisfied.

Emily (Pearce) Tilley, 82 years old at the time of our conversation, told me of an incident which occurred when she was having her family. During one of her pregnancies she recalled that she was walking along the road in Maberly one day when she met a male neighbour. He was carrying a salmon. Salmon was a delicacy, a change of fare from codfish, and perhaps he did not wish to part with any. Fearful that she would crave some, he put the salmon down his trouser leg, out of sight till she passed by. However, when she heard about his fear some time later, she found it rather funny, as she had had no special craving during either of her pregnancies and did not believe that unsatisfied cravings caused "birthmarks."

On another occasion, she said, an older woman brought her some fresh meat (only obtainable when someone slaughtered a cow, or goat, etc.) with orders to cook it because "I've been a dru it" (i.e., I've been through it myself and I'm sure you'd like a little of this.) The older woman just naturally assumed that the pregnant woman would crave something special like fresh meat. Although this informant had had no cravings herself, she did know many women who reported having had them. She said a sure indication to the neighbourhood that one woman was expecting again was her visit to a neighbour's to obtain some pickled cabbage (cabbage kept over the winter in salt pickle). Another desired baked beans and brown bread. These women were always given the foods they desired as soon as their wishes were known.

A woman in her forties told me that when she was born she had a birthmark on her eye shaped like a black currant. Her mother told her that while she was carrying her she had had an unsatisfied craving for this fruit. Nearly every day she would pass by the garden where the black currants she desired grew, but she didn't feel like helping herself to any of the fruit, nor did she feel like asking the owner of the garden for some of the berries. However, after Hester was born with the black currant-shaped mark on her eye, the mother confided in the woman who owned the garden and the latter said: "You'll have some if that'll do any good." And, said my informant, "Mother went and got the black currants and stewed 'um. And she gave me the juice on a spoon, and afterwards the birthmark disappeared."[5] She added: "Even today I feel that as long as I've got jam in the house, I feel like well . . . I've got everything there. If I get out of jam I'm always hungry."

If the child escaped being marked because of its mother's unsatisfied craving, it would more than likely be born with a craving for that food. Another woman, Rhoda Pearce, recalled how before her second child was born she visited a home where they were having blueberry cake for supper. She would have liked a piece, but wouldn't think of asking for it because it was considered "bad manners" to do so. And apparently the neighbour didn't think that something so ordinary as blueberry cake would be "craved," so she didn't offer her any. Later, when her son was born, he cried a great deal for the first few weeks, and finally her mother-in-law, with whom she was living at the time, asked her if there had been anything she had craved and had not got. Learning about the blueberry cake, she got some blueberries, stewed them and gave the baby some of the juice. This cured him, for from then on he began to thrive and did not cry without a reason.

Apparently, if the mother got what she craved before the birth, the child would neither be marked nor have the same craving for the food his mother desired. Sarah Chaulk said that her next-door neighbour had a great desire for oranges before the birth of her first child. Oranges were hard to get at that time, some forty to fifty years ago, but just before her time she got a half dozen. So ravenous was she, said Mrs. Chaulk, that "she ate half a dozen, skins and all!" The boy had no particular desire for the fruit. This woman also told me about her niece who craved apples during her pregnancy. Since the niece worked in their grocery store, she could easily satisfy her craving and ate apples ravenously until her daughter was born. The child had only a normal liking for apples.

The physical causes of birthmarks were harder to predict and often it was only after the child was born that the mother would think on what had caused the mark. I heard of one case where a birthmark on a child's face was explained by the fact of his mother's being startled by being hit in the face by a mitten that had been playfully thrown at her. Another child had a round black birthmark on the top of her head. Her family believed that it was the result of her mother's striking the top of her head on the oven door before the child's birth.

Even such things as mental retardation might be blamed on something that happened to the mother during her pregnancy. It was believed that if the mother suffered a bad fright or a "turn," her child would be retarded. And this was the case only twelve years ago when a pregnant woman was frightened by an angry dog's jumping on her. Her child, born a little while later, was badly retarded and the fright was believed to have caused it. Of course such an incident could not have been predicted. However a woman need not purposely risk such a fate for her child by looking at a dead body, for many people believed that a pregnant woman should not look at anyone dead as:

"she might get a fright, a turn. It'd give 'um something, they say that something 'd be into 'm you know, if the mother gets a bad fright," said Sarah Chaulk.[6]

Physical deformities might be caused by a physical act such as a fall or the cause might be a psychological one — punishment for bad behaviour. A fall, especially in the later stages of pregnancy, when a woman was "well on" was, of course, recognized as very dangerous. One woman said that her granddaughter "fell down and had alike to kill herself, before she had the youngster." The child died soon after its birth. "It had no brains." The grandmother believed this condition was due to the mother's bad fall.

More rarely physical defects, like a crippled arm or leg, were said to result from the mother's mocking of an afflicted person. When I was a child I remember being told by my mother that it used to be said that a certain person in the community was badly crippled because of the terrible thing his mother did before he was born: she mocked (made fun of) a crippled person. Her own similarly crippled child was believed to be her punishment.[7] Years later, I heard that the child had not been born a cripple, but had had an attack of infantile paralysis while just a tiny baby. To ridicule persons less fortunate than one's self was considered a terrible sin and children especially had to be thoroughly warned of the possible consequences. The older folk obviously took pretty seriously the commandment about "the sins of the fathers being visited on the children."

People wise in such matters would judge from a pregnant woman's shape whether the newcomer would be a boy or a girl. If a woman were bigger in front she might expect a girl; if the behind had it, a boy. One informant, Sarah Chaulk, said the signs were right in her case, but Jane Pearce, who bore eleven children, said there was nothing in it.

Although some of my informants were quite voluble, others were almost Victorian in their treatment of the subject of pregnancy, especially if any male were present. For instance, they would make vague motions indicating where a woman might expect to "show" most, depending on whether she was carrying a girl or boy baby. None of them used crude language in referring to the matter. Perhaps such a "prim and proper" attitude is not so surprising when one realizes that when these women were having babies such matters were only discussed in guarded terms among women, and rarely, if ever, in mixed company.

"Borning babies" was women's work. There might be a number of women around, but no men. Said William Crewe, now in his eighties and father of eleven children: "Did they think we knew nothing about it, for gracious sake?" Men were banished from the premises while a baby was being born. All the father could do was hurry off for the midwife and get her to the house in time.

Home confinement was the accepted practice well into the 1940s; the room used depended on home circumstances and the weather. Ordinarily the child was born in an upstairs bedroom as practically all the homes were two-storey structures. In some cases the birth might take place in the "inside place," i.e., the parlour, or even in the kitchen. Mother and baby had to be kept warm. In those days before central heating and portable electric heaters, upstairs rooms could be extremely cold in the wintertime. Usually only the kitchen and parlour had a stove; sometimes just the former room. However some households had smelly portable kerosene heaters that might be used in cold weather.

Children who were at the inquisitive age might be sent off to stay with relatives or neighbours till the new baby had arrived. One of my younger informants, Nina Pearce, a woman in her forties, recalled that when a younger sister of hers was born, her mother was confined in the inside place which was underneath the room where she slept. There was a hatchway in the ceiling of the inside place to permit warm air to rise to the bedroom above. She said she lay down on the floor and glued her eyes to the opening in order to see what was taking place in the room below. However she soon fell asleep and awoke to find that the baby had arrived. She belonged to the generation which believed that babies were brought in the midwife's black bag.[8] When she got the chance she opened the bag and was disappointed to find it only held some scissors and a bit of string! I remember "Granny" Trask's black bag but I never had the courage to sneak a look inside. The "put-off" my older informants had received when they asked where they had come from was that they had been found "in the cellar."[9] A cellar was ordinarily a cave hollowed into the side of a hill. The outer walls were of rock. The roof was a wooden framework covered with sods. It was always dark and cool, ideal for the storage of vegetables.

Children in the Maberly-Neck section of Elliston were told that babies came from a particular cellar: "John Murphy's Cellar." Mr. Murphy's wife, Sarah or Aunt Sally, was the midwife there when most of my older informants were born. One of them, my Aunt Hilda, at the age of five or six happened to go to this cellar, and after studying it for a while she came to the conclusion: "This is an awful small cellar for Aunt Sally Murphy to find all those babies in." People from the main section of Elliston were simply told: "in the cellar."

It was a midwife who brought most of the children into the world. Sometimes there were two practicing at the same period and of course help was always forthcoming from older women if the need arose. None of these women had any particular training other than that supplied by experience. Speaking of them, Jane Pearce said:

> What did they know about it, Hilda, at all? They never had nar bit o' learnin' (i.e., medical training), did they? Suzy Randell had nar bit o' learnin' nor Jane Trask didn't.

Then she reminisced about the time some twenty to thirty years before when she had "helped born" a young neighbour's baby.

> If we hadn't done for X . . . . she'd have been dead when he [the doctor] came, he said so himself. He said, if she'd had to wait till he came she'd have been dead before he got here.

Another woman, Orpah Crewe, remembered the midwives who attended her as being kind old ladies. However,

> when she [the midwife] was on a case, all hands went by the midwife. Her word was law. She did just the same as the doctor, you see, in her own way. Oh, they were good too, maid. They were good people, old ladies.

Mentioning their equipment, she said:

> They had their bit of twine in their bag, bit of white twine, and their scissors, in the little bag. That's all.

The midwife did no housework. Her job was to attend to the baby and the mother and to:

> get a cup of tea for the patient and a cup for herself. They'd stay in all night if you was sick in the night . . . Stay all the night and the next day. But if she came early in the morning probably she'd go back that night if there was anybody else . . . you know . . . expectin' to be sick [in labour]. She'd go back so's they . . . or the man'd come in here for her.

"And 'twas tough gettin' the old lady back and forth them times, I'll tell the world!" said William Crewe. In winter she might be brought on horse and sleigh or dog sled; in summer, by horse and buggy. Often she walked perhaps two or three miles. Sometimes she was sent for during a raging blizzard. One woman discussing the birth of her first child recalled how she was then living with her in-laws, her husband being away working in the lumberwoods. She was young, about nineteen, and rather shy, and she didn't know how to convey to her mother-in-law how she felt. However, the old lady wasn't blind and seeing how matters stood, she dispatched her husband and son-in-law, living nearby, for the midwife who lived approximately two miles away.

> Off they went with a dog slide and twas so rough, look you was not able to see a picket [paling fence] out there [indicating a distance of about twenty feet] for the snow. And twas still gettin' worse you see. That was Saturday and they went off before dark and never got back till the mornin' nearly. Stark rough, couldn't see nothin' . . . Now I didn't know but that I'd want a doctor and no one didn't know. And if I'd wanted a doctor I'd a died.

Describing the midwife's arrival in the home she said:

> They came right in the porch with her, and she was nothig but a snowbank. Had her head and all covered right over, smothered! And I was all that night [i.e., in labour] till four o'clock in the morning . . . .

This was the sort of situation the midwife often faced. Should a doctor's services be required, an attempt would be made to get him, but he was five to seven miles away and getting him in time for a so-called "doctor's case" was practically an impossibility. If the midwife arrived early enough and foresaw a difficult birth, she would have the doctor sent for at once. This happened to Sarah Chaulk whose only son was born in late December. She had the less experienced midwife in attendance, the chief one being involved with another case elsewhere in the community. Both she and her husband were thankful that they did have the junior because she was more fearful and "wouldn't drive things out" as the more confident older woman might have. The midwife advised that the doctor be sent for, and getting him from Bonavista to Maberly, a distance of seven miles, proved no problem for the weather was just marvellous that evening. By the time he was ready to leave Maberly however, a howling blizzard was raging and when it was over the snow was well over the fences. Getting the doctor back to Bonavista exhausted all the young father's ingenuity. They used horse and sleigh, dog team and slide, and finally "shank's mare." It was a risk to be expecting a baby in midwinter in those days! But if the weather remained good, it was considered by many women the best time, for a woman would not be rushed with her many chores as she would be in the summertime and she might spend a whole month upstairs recuperating, as long as there was someone to handle the housework. Usually the new grandmother would be pleased to take care of this for her daughter.

In very early times it seems that in summer women worked to the very last minute before the baby was born. Maud Hobbs, spoke thus of her mother's generation:

> They worked till the last minute. Aunt A . . . H . . . used to tell me that she had to leave the stage one time and go up and go to bed and have a baby, and she had the scales on her hands [i.e., fish scales]. She didn't have time to wash her hands!

The informant's husband added: "Lots of cases like that when the child was born in fishin' time. Fishermen's wives you see."

Jane Pearce, who reared eleven children during the depression period of the 1930s, could speak for that period of time also:

> . . . in the gardens and the children to do for, and I had to make bread and I was bad enough. And I made bread, maid, and I was lookin' about their clothes to see how they wuz, sewing all night long you know, fraid I would take sick [i.e., go into labour] in the middle of the night.

And she spoke of "working down below," at the fish on the flake and in the stage, with the perspiration rolling off her.

> That's how twas. Now sure, there's no tear on nothing now [tear, working at everything]. Nobody has to work so hard anymore.

The midwives were very fearful lest their patients take a chill or get childbed fever. Mrs. Pearce related how crazy she would be for some cold water when she'd hear the rattle of buckets as someone prepared to go to the well for a "turn" of water. But she wouldn't be given a drop. A cup of tea or some warm drink was all she was allowed. Neither did the midwives think too highly of the virtues of fresh air. Mary Jane Porter, whose first child was born in August in the 1930s, wanted her window open after the child was born. She succeeded in having this done, but the midwife warned her that she wouldn't take the blame should anything happen because of this foolishness.

The normal time a new mother was expected to stay in bed was ten days. Some, whose families could not get along without the mother's services for so long, were at the regular grind just a few days after the birth. Others, with the first child especially, might not take up regular duties for a month, particularly if the birth occurred in the winter.

Traditionally in Elliston the tenth day after the birth was the mother's "Up-sitting Day." For this special occasion a relative, or someone in the house, made a special cake called the "Groaning Cake" and other dainty fare if the larder could afford it. They tried to have something a bit different from the ordinary food, although sometimes just raisin bread served as the Groaning Cake. Most certainly raisins had to be used. On the afternoon of the Up-sitting Day the neighbour women would drop in and the midwife would come back to the house. All would sit around the kitchen table and would enjoy a cup of tea and some of the Groaning Cake. Some would get to see the new baby for the first time at this little social gathering, but usually the group was composed of women who had been present at the birth.

The custom of having a Groaning Cake after the birth of a child is widely reported from England, though the only West Country reference is from Cornwall. Reverend George Patterson indicated that in Newfoundland the Groaning Cake was prepared in anticipation of a birth, and after it had taken place distributed to those present at a feast.[10] This does not agree with findings in Elliston where it was not made in advance. This would, I suspect, have been considered a presumptuous thing to do. Neither was the cake distributed soon after the birth, but was served at a special get together on the woman's Up-sitting Day.

Orpah Crew remembered the ritual of Up-sitting Day:

They used to bake a raisin bread for the day you'd get up. They called that your Up-sitting Day, see. You know, the woman'd get up and they'd always have a bread, and they had short cake baked and a pie, they might have had that, but the main Groaning Cake was raisin bread.

89

She recalled her Up-sitting Day as being the third day after the birth rather than the tenth:

> When the baby was born they'd come in that day for a cup of tea. All would sit around the table, five or six ladies you know, and Mrs. Trask or Mrs. Randell, whoever was there . . . Somebody'd tend table. My poor old mother most commonly 'd tend table for me, you know. Nice, maid, you'd never believe. Use'n have nothing special you see. Only the cup of tea and the raisin bread and the pie or old-fashioned tart, we'll call it. A few buns. Twas nice. A lot better than tis now. Twas nice, comfortable. Your labour was over, we'll say and your child was born . . . Everything was okay. You enjoyed it and . . . .

It would seem that those women who observed the traditional Up-sitting Day thought of it as one way of expressing their thanks for a safe delivery. They were happy to have the travail behind them and wished to have their friends around them to rejoice with them. Besides it was a sort of "thank-you" to those women who helped at the birth.

The custom was not strong in all parts of the community. Maud Hobbs, now in her eighties, had only one child, a girl. She did not remember having a cup of tea with friends, but she remembered that her mother-in-law had made a special cake at the time though she didn't know what she called it:

> I remember her saying to Joe 'Go out and bring me in some raisins to make a cake for that maid'.

By the time today's young matrons were having babies the custom of having a Groaning Cake had died out. Those who were older children from larger families, however, remember their mothers' cup of tea, although they are not too sure of the terms. Nina Pearce said:

> Mom and they had it. The tenth day they'd get up. They'd always have a bit of cake or something baked and ask in all the crowd around . . . In those days they'd always have a cup of tea. The midwife she'd come in on that day. If she was gone home she'd come back that tenth day . . . They used to call it "Up-sit Cake" or "Sitting-Up Cake" or something like that. Something like that they used to call it, cause Dad used to bake 'um for Mom. Dad was the real

hand to bake cakes. He'd always bake 'um for Mom.

Both Up-Sitting Day and Groaning Cake are definitely English traditions. The former seems to be associated with christening and according to the *Oxford English Dictionary* is a word peculiar to Exmoor (North Deven/West Somerset). It is not listed in the *English Dialect Dictionary*. The Newfoundland Dictionary Centre has no reference in its files to Up-Sitting Day but there are New England references to "setting up" visits being made and special cakes being eaten at the time.[11]

The Groaning Cake in Elliston was never the same thing as the christening cake, although apparently this was the case in a few sections of Newfoundland.[12]

Christening, the next major event for the mother, was kept quite separate from Up-sitting Day and took place according to the traditions of the different denominations in the community. By 1900 there were three of these: Anglican, Methodist (United Church), and Salvation Army. The few adherents to the Roman Catholic faith had either died, moved away, or become converted to the dominant church in the community, the Methodist.

The tradition with which I am best acquainted is that of the Anglican Church, and it was from Anglican informants that most of my information about christening came. All Anglican children were taken to church to be christened. This, in normal cases, usually took place about a month after the child's birth. If the child were sickly, however, baptism would be administered at home by some responsible person, perhaps the local school teacher. Sometime later the child would be taken to the church or school chapel and "received into the congregation," but "no water would be used on him there if he had been privately baptised." A boy had two godfathers and one godmother; a girl had two godmothers and one godfather. Before the 1920s it seems there was no hard and fast rule in the Elliston Anglican church regarding who could be godparents to a child. Emily (Pearce) Tilley told me that when her children were being baptised the godparents did not have to be "confirmed" persons, that is confirmed in the Anglican Church. In fact one of her children's sponsors was a Methodist. Some of those godparents in the early days who were strict "Church" people took the baptismal vows they made very seriously and saw to it that the godchild was duly confirmed. Later on, although the rule became more rigid about who could be godparents, outside interference by the godparents in such private matters as the religious training of the child would not have been tolerated, and many children today, even those born in the thirties, do not know who their godparents were.

It was a common saying in Elliston as in other parts of the world that a child who cries at his christening will have a long life.[13] One informant recalled that her daughter, normally quiet, kicked up quite a fuss. She cried till she was taken home. In spite of the saying about "long life" most mothers would feel embarrassed if their babies were noisy during church service. For ordinarily the christening took place midway through the normal Sunday service, matins, or evensong, and there might be several babies to be christened. To keep the baby quiet during the ceremony mothers carried along a "sugar tit." This was some sugar wrapped in muslin and greatly resembled the "blueing rag" used on wash day. When the baby had a sugar tit stuffed in his mouth, he couldn't yell too loudly.

Boys and girls were always christened in a special "christening dress." This was often made by hand of some "good white material," trimmed with handmade lace and very long. In some families the christening dress was handed down through the different generations, and of course if one were made for the christening of the first child in the family it would be used for all other children in that family. Often those who had no christening dress borrowed from a better-off neighbour. Sometimes, I believe, the dress was further trimmed by having attached at the shoulders a blue satin bow to indicate a boy, or a pink one to indicate a girl.

In my own family tradition I am accustomed to a get together on the occasion of the christening of the first child. Some of the wedding cake was saved for the "first" christening, or if the wedding cake had several tiers, the small top cake was saved in its entirety. I do not know how widespread the custom might be as none of my informants mentioned it. However, it is customary to have christening cakes in other parts of Newfoundland.

The subject of christening did not come up with my United Church informants. Perhaps this is because it was customary until within the last twenty to thirty years for Methodist babies to be christened in their homes by the minister, the parents being their child's sponsors. Some of the older very strict "Church" people might even argue that Salvation Army babies who were dedicated in the Army and not "properly baptised" with water, were not even Christians! Imagine the situation the Anglican priest in the community found himself in after conducting a full burial service for an adult worshipper in the Anglican Church who, as a baby had been dedicated in the Salvation Army and had never been baptised! If an Anglican child died before baptism he would be buried in the graveyard, but without the formal burial service. In the early nineteenth century it seems such children were buried in unconsecrated ground, for I have been told recently that such a child was buried in a garden in Maberly, although there is nothing marking the site of the grave.

The name a child received at his christening in the old days was very likely a Biblical one. Mary, often nicknamed "Polly," was common for girls, and there were many double names like Mary Hannah, Mary Ann, Mary Jane, etc. Quite often it happened that there were several persons bearing the same name living near each other. At one time there were seven men bearing the name James Porter. To distinguish between them people called them by various nicknames, including Shoemaker Jim, Soldier Jim, Brook Jim, Little Jim, etc. Some religious people were not content with simple Biblical names like Joseph or Peter, or Thomas, and chose instead strange sounding ones like Vashti, Tabitha, Nehemiah, Hezekiah, Gideon, Amaziah, Archelaus, and Nimshi. An old lady once inquired of my mother what another woman had named her twins, a boy and a girl. On being told: Adolphus and Anastacia, she exclaimed:

I'll never be able to tell Jim them names. I'll have to say she called 'um Duff and Stach.

Finding suitable names must have been a problem for most parents since big families were the rule. A dozen children or more per family was not uncommon in the early part of the century though by the 1950s such large families were no longer popular. Birth control methods were apparently frowned on. As Maud Hobbs put it:

They'd be having babies every two years. [It was] the Lord's will. That was their family. That's the way they looked at it then you know.

My Aunt Hilda, youngest in a family of six, also remarked on the size of families in the old days, saying that theirs was a small family by the standards of the time, the usual run being a dozen or more.

Of course, with the great amount of work to be done, a large family was a necessity. Children were an important part of the economy for, as soon as they could handle jobs around the house, the garden, or "down below," they were expected to help. For the most part I suspect that as in the early days in New England:

93

These large families were eagerly welcomed. Children were a blessing. The Danish proverb says, "Children are the poor man's wealth." To the farmer, especially the frontiersman, every child in the home is an extra producer.[14]

The newborn child, however, meant extra work for the mother and older girls in the family. When he was not sharing his mother's arms or her bed, or being carried around by other members, he spent a fair amount of his daytime hours in a cradle. This was homemade of wood with sloping sides and perhaps a wooden canopy at the head. It was mounted on rockers. Inside it might be furnished with a small feather bed, but often there were simply heavy pieces of material folded up for a mattress, and there would likely be a small pillow. Emily (Pearce) Tilley told me that she had a special "swinging cradle" for her children. Her husband made it.

Cribs, common in the community now, are a comparatively recent introduction. Most babies and toddlers shared their parents' bed at night, especially during the wintertime. It was the only way to assure that they would stay covered up and cosy when the frost sparkled on the window panes and could be flaked off with a finger nail. Besides, ofttimes during the winter, the man of the house was away for several months working, usually in the lumberwoods. Then the younger members of the family always slept with mother, with some "sleeping at the foot of the bed."

An expression often used about young children was: "Pretty in the cradle, ugly at the table." Or, "Ugly in the cradle, pretty at the table."[15] The first could stop someone from gushing too much about a new baby, and the second could console a mother whose child seemed plain and homely-looking.

Although many homes kept cats as pets, most mothers were very careful of tiny babies when cats were present. They would never let a cat sleep in the baby's cradle for fear they said "that the cat would take the child's breath."[16]

Sarah Chaulk remembered how careful they were over the heads of newborn babies:

You're not allowed to do nothing with the skull, the soft part. Not allowed to do nothing with that or comb until tis solid . . . Even a brush or cloth . . . for three months.

To prevent what they called "cradle crap" they would keep olive oil on this section and

> go over it with a linen rag. Didn't comb there till twas hard. Soft, twouldn' growed see.

Every newborn baby had to wear a "belly band." This was a two-inch wide strip of flannelette which was bound tightly around the child's body covering the bellybutton. It was kept on for two or three weeks. "If they didn't, something wrong," continued Mrs. Chaulk.

Sometimes children were born with what was called "white mouth." The midwife's cure for this was to put molasses on the child's tongue. "They would use a little piece of clean linen and wipe the molasses around inside the mouth and the molasses would cut it all off," Sarah Chaulk told me.[17]

Babies did not get their hair cut until they were at least a year old and some mothers whose little boys had lovely curly hair might try to preserve the ringlets longer than that. Also, some people in the community considered it unlucky to cut a child's fingernails during the first year, and to avoid this bad luck, they bit the nails off. However no one mentioned the common belief held elsewhere that the child might become a thief if his fingernails were cut off during the first year.[18]

For difficult teething there were no jellies or drops as can be purchased nowadays. The most common aid for babies cutting their teeth was hardtack. This hard biscuit was in everyone's pantry and had the added advantage that it could be eaten; hence, nearly all teething babies would be given scraps of hard bread to chew on.

Mothers whose children had an especially difficult time teething often resorted to special "charms" (amulets). One of these beliefs has survived down to the present day. The "charm" was a necklace made from part of a lobster shell. My informants varied on exactly which parts were used. Some said the feelers; others said the small legs. But all agreed that the charm worked. Joyce Porter, a teenager now, had a difficult time cutting her teeth. A neighbour brought the mother the "necklace" her children had used. In this case the lobster shell was covered with some cloth. They put on some fresh material and put the charm on the child's neck. From then on "we broke no more rest because of her teething," stated her grandmother, Mary Jane Porter. In earlier days it was also a common sight to see a baby wearing a small silver Newfoundland five-cent piece attached to his wrist by a piece of ribbon or string. This could be rubbed on the gums, said those who called it a teething charm.[19] Others said it was simply a good-luck charm.

There was not the array of oils, powders, soaps, and lotions to choose from in the period 1900–1940 as there is today. Most of my informants used burnt flour to dust babies' bottoms with. To prevent the baby's buttocks getting sore, or to cure diaper rash, they would line the regular flannelette diaper with a piece of material that had been scorched on the hot stove and sprinkle on burnt flour for powder. Rhoda Pearce mentioned that she kept this burnt flour in a can and sprinkled it just as we would baby powder nowadays.

Until the 1950s and perhaps later, most of the baby's layette — diapers, shirts, wrappers, sleepers, etc. — were made from soft flannelette. The mother and grandmother usually made these by hand, or by machine if one were available. However there were no printed patterns for any item; they had to follow the outline of some previous garment, or work "by guess and by God."

The clothing one had on hand for the newborn might affect its future.[20] Some women believed that it was quite all right to have everything ready beforehand, except any sort of head covering. According to Sarah Chaulk, it was considered unlucky to make a cap or any kind of bonnet before the child was born.

Newborn babies did not enjoy the freedom of movement that today's babies have. They could not "kick and fling" as they wished. Winter and summer, children were bound up in "whittles,"[21] night and day, for two or three months at least, though after this period they were given more freedom of movement during the day. Putting a child in "whittles" or "whetals" was also termed "dressing them up for the night." "They were like a stick nightime," said Annie Chaulk.

First a baby was dressed in a triangular flannelette diaper. Over this went large "pieces" very much like quilts, thick and absorbent, so that no wetness could come through to the unprotected bed. Then "a great, big, long night dress" and an outside "wrapper," the front of which was often worked in some bright yarn. The pieces and wrapper were doubled up around the child's feet and fastened at the waist. Even after he was "shortened," i.e., didn't have the clothing doubled up over his feet, a baby was still dressed in thick "pieces" plus his diaper at night, until he was toilet trained. After the child was "dressed-up" for the night he was not unbound until the morning, and, of course, every morning the baby's whittles had to be washed. Drying such thick pieces presented quite a problem when the weather was wet and cold. By the 1940s there was not the same need for these whittles for thin rubber sheets were available for the protection of bedding. However this was an expense that few parents could afford during the Depression years, so the whittles stayed until economic conditions were somewhat improved.

Boys were usually kept in dresses till they were a year old at least, and some were three or four before they were put in rompers and short pants. Several informants said boys were dressed in this manner because "it was just the fashion." However Sarah Chaulk said that it was believed that "if they were not kept in dresses it made them dirty." Hence one reason for letting boys go around dressed in what to us nowadays seems a "sissy" fashion, was this practical one; it was a timesaver for the busy mother or maid.

Almost without exception children were breast fed, and some women were not very hygienic in their feeding practices. Emily (Pearce) Tilley said that when she herself was just a baby in the cradle, a neighbour woman picked her up and nursed her while her mother was out. She wondered why she did not catch tuberculosis, because the woman's husband was found to be a carrier of this disease. Even at the time she herself was having babies, during the 1920s, conditions were not much better in some homes. She said:

> Children were not cared for at all. Simply rocked in a cradle with perhaps a sugar tit to suck on.

When children were given solid food, it was not an uncommon sight, she said, to have mothers chewing up the food to give to their babies, instead of letting it soak in milk. She was fiercely against this practice and tried to get those women to do otherwise.

Another woman also recalled that babies "were not looked after like they are now." Very few were reared on the bottle and they did not get solid food for a long time. She mentioned that "babies were fed with the fingers, and the old people were worse than that!" She did not explain this. Despite such treatment a surprising number lived, judging from the size of the families.

Only those women who were incapable of breast feeding their children resorted to bottle feeding, for in the early days and even in the thirties, this was an intricate proceeding. The feeding bottle was of glass, "fitted with a big, long, glass tube and a glass quill on the end," then the nipple. This contraption had to be cleaned in salt and water. The milk given infants was usually the condensed, sweetened variety; Eagle and Purity were two brands mentioned. Cow's milk was also given. In some cases where the child did not seem to thrive on cow's milk or if he had some childhood disease like measles, goat's milk was usually suggested as being better for him. Most of the goats in the community were kept because their milk was recommended for the infants in the family. My father bought our first goat after my brother Albert had had the measles.

Mothers varied on the times when they gave their children the first solid food. Some gave it at two-three months; others didn't give any until the child was at least a year old. Undoubtedly it depended to a great extent on the quantity and richness of the maternal milk supply. Baby food in tins, with which we are now so familiar, did not appear in markets until within very recent years, but cereals like Pablum and Cream of Wheat have been around for quite a while. Sarah Chaulk, whose son was born in the 1920s, mentioned that she used "Nestlé's Food." This came in "a big, round can" and was sufficient for three to four months. This, like the tinned milk she used, was sweetened. Such baby food was only obtained through the doctor's offices.

Having a young baby to care for was not considered a reason for the mother to shirk her many outdoor duties. Watching over the baby became the responsibility of the older girl or girls in the family, or the child was cared for by a hired nursemaid. The latter might be the young daughter of a next-door neighbour who would come by day. People who were slightly better off might employ a "servant-girl" to care for the baby and be responsible for much of the indoor work. For, as noted in Chapter Three, a girl undertook responsibilities at a very early age which prepared her for her future role in the community.

# Chapter 6
# The Woman and Her Home

In addition to helping with making a living, and bearing and rearing children, a woman was responsible for running the home. The extent and nature of her household duties was determined to a great degree by the house she lived in.

Within living memory each family in Elliston has lived in the one house all year round. It seems likely though, that in the early days of settlement in Elliston, some families may have moved away from the exposed coast during the winter, returning to their fishing base in summer. Since there is a "Tilt Path" about three miles up the shore from Maberly and about two miles inland, in a very sheltered area, there must have been a "tilt" or "tilts" there for the spot to get such a name. Elliston fishermen, unlike many in Bonavista, lived comparatively close to the shore and their fishing premises. In Bonavista, only five miles away, "transhumance" (the movement from winter to summer quarters and vice-versa) was quite common even in recent times. Some fishermen in Bonavista, even in the 1940s, maintained fishing premises "down on the Cape," but lived in Bonavista three miles away during the winter. They moved to their summer houses for the duration of the fishing season. Other Bonavista residents lived in permanent homes in Bonavista except for two or three months of the winter when they went "in the Bay" or "up on the Line" where wood was plentiful. Here they lived in small, one-room, rough timber shacks, called "tilts". During the two or three month period they cut their firewood for the year as well as wood for building purposes.

Most of the older people I talked with were of the opinion that while the majority of the early houses in Elliston were small, nearly all were two stories, though the second storey was probably very low-ceilinged. The consensus was that the commonest old-style house was the one known in New England as the "saltbox." This had a "gable" or peaked roof with a short side toward the front and a long side sloping down to just a few feet above the ground at the back. Homes built in this fashion were still common in Elliston in the 1920s; by the 1940s there were just a few. Today only one remains unchanged and inhabited.

Another house style mentioned was that with a "cottage roof." This also was small and two-storied; the roof had four equally sloping sides. Very few of this type remain in their original form in Elliston. In nearly all houses the ceilings were low by today's standards, no more than six or six and a half feet high. Upstairs' ceilings were, of course, affected by the shape of the roof; they were very low at the back of the house even on the ground storey under the long roof of the "salt box."

My Aunt Hilda once told me that when she was teaching in a small community in Bonavista Bay she was surprised to find a family still living in a house with a sod roof. Sod roofs were common enough on root cellars in Elliston, but no one I talked with could remember seeing any house in Elliston with a sod roof; nor had they heard of any. Early Elliston house roofs had wooden shingles on them. All early houses were built of "studs," i.e., 2″ x 4″ timbers, roughed out with an axe. These were placed upright, side by side, to form the walls. The narrow spaces between the studs were "chinched" with moss and wood shavings, or anything that would keep out the drafts. Some of these "studded" houses were clapboarded outside and the inside was boarded up or "ceiled" with very wide boards, sawn with a "pit-saw" since there were no sawmills near at hand. The clapboard was painted if the family could afford paint. If not, they whitewashed the clapboard, but usually painted the "corner pieces" and windows red or brown.

During the first decade of the twentieth century, roof styles changed. Carpenters who built peaked roof houses at this time made both sides of the gable roof the same length. Now ceilings upstairs could be of uniform height and, in addition, there was space for an attic or "top loft," directly under the roof, which could be used for storage. The idea caught on, and when a man needed to repair the roof of his oldstyle house, he frequently changed it to a roof having gables of equal length.

Another roof style in common use from about 1910 onwards was the "flat-roof." This roof was not actually horizontal, but the slope was not very great. "Felt," i.e., tar paper, was used to cover this type of roof. The flat-roofed and gable-roofed houses are the two house styles that have persisted till the present day. It is only within recent years that the modern one-storey "bungalow" has been built.

Of course the better-off families usually had much larger homes than other people. And at all times some individuals built houses that differed markedly in style from the majority. Some homes were built with "mansard" roofs; others had gable or cottage roofs with dormer windows. In still others, the windows at the front were protruding or "bay windows." The majority of older homes, however, had one style of window:

> These were small compared to the standard now with nine panes in each window. The window shades were made of white material called shirting which had to be washed often and starched; they were rolled by hand, no springs. Sometimes there was a valance at the top of the window.

Apart from roof styles and the kind and number of windows, houses also varied in other ways. For instance, the majority had only one chimney, built at one end, but some homes had chimneys at both ends.

Some of the older, poorer houses, built just after stoves came into use (perhaps 1870s), had no chimney. Instead a stove pipe went up through the roof. This was in three or four foot lengths and could be taken apart for cleaning. Then there was a length of pipe attached to a flange which was nailed to the roof. The stovepipe warmed the bedroom upstairs through which it passed. Behind the stove downstairs was a piece of heavy tin to keep the wall from scorching. Many of the older homes did have chimneys though and several of my informants spoke of the big wide chimney which was built of rock to the roof. This part of the chimney was referred to as "the back." Only the part projecting on the roof, built of brick, was the "chimbly." In some homes the chimney or flue which had accomodated the open fire was modified to suit stoves. Only one person, Edwin Baker, could remember an open fireplace. It must have been one of the last of them: the one in use at Thomas Tilly's place.

"I remember the open fireplace," he said, "the flue with the crooks and crottles for hanging pots on." The "crook and crottles" was shaped not unlike a walking stick with a hook which went over the iron bar that stretched across the open fireplace. It had one straight side and the other side was notched. The whole hung down from the horizontal iron bar and could be slid along it. Pots could be raised or lowered on the crottles according to the housewife's desires. "They'd start the pot boiling near the open fire then they'd shift it up a notch." Cooking would then continue at a normal rate.

Every house had a "bridge", often two, one at the front door and one at the back, but they varied from house to house. A bridge might mean a wooden platform extending from the doorway and ascended by a step or two, or it might simply be steps leading up to the door. Some of the "better" homes had "galleries" (verandas) which ran the full width of the front of the house. Nearly every house in Elliston by the 1900s had a front door and front steps.

Elliston homes did not have what I have heard jokingly called in various communities the "mother-in-law" door. This is a front door which is several feet above the ground with no steps leading from it. All front doors were kept tightly closed during the winter but were occasionally used during the summer months. Ordinarily, entrance to the house was through the back door. Most people went through the back porch to the kitchen. Only the minister or important strangers entered the house through the front door. My mother often told me that when Canon Bayly visited his parishioners and entered a house by the front door, he always made sure that he went out the same way. He considered it unlucky to do otherwise and should he start to go out the "wrong" way he would come back and go out the "right" way.

In the old days no houses had basements though some were laid on stronger foundations than others. The majority had rock walls cemented together for the foundations; others just perched on columns of rock placed at regular intervals. Usually though, this space was filled in because it made the house warmer. The house site was generally a spot that was of little use for gardening purposes as good land was scarce. Little attention seems to have been paid to the view or to the direction in which the house faced. Not infrequently the front door faced away from the main road and it was the back door which was nearest the road. The main consideration for the house site was its closeness to the man's work at the fishing premises.

Many young men began building their own homes when only in their teens, sometimes years before they were thinking about marriage, or had even begun serious courting. Building a house was a slow process; it might take years. Often if the man were handy with tools, he did most of

102

the work. This meant he could only work at it out of the fishing season — in the late fall or early winter — and then only when the weather prevented him from going five or ten miles in the "woods" for fuel. Some young men, perhaps better fixed financially, preferred to have a qualified carpenter build the house. There was, however, very little discussion on the shape and style of the house and no blueprints. The carpenter built the type of house he himself fancied and was responsible for all aspects of the building. He had free rein, for often the owner was away in the lumberwoods earning the money to pay for the house.

Wives or women in the family had no more say on how the house should be built or laid out than the girl who married a man from Elliston who had his house built long before he married. His favourite answer to those who teased him was, "You got to have the cage before you can get the bird." It is doubtful that the woman's plans would have deviated much from the norm anyway, unless she had spent some time elsewhere and had become used to another house layout that she liked better. Probably when she moved into the house she might persuade her husband to make some changes. My Aunt Hilda recalled that when she and her mother and sister moved into the new house built by her two older brothers, they found the kitchen area to be far too small. Very soon a porch was added across the end of the house extending the kitchen to the needed size.

In spite of exterior variations, the floor plan upstairs and down was the same in most older Elliston homes. There were two main rooms downstairs, plus a pantry and porch. The most important of these rooms was the kitchen; the other downstairs room was usually a parlour, but sometimes it was used as a bedroom. A few homes had separate dining rooms in addition to the parlour or "inside place." Generally a small hallway separated the parlour and the kitchen, and from it the stairs, usually "box stairs," ascended to the four small rooms above. In the small minority of homes with no front door, this hallway was called "the staircase"; otherwise the hallway was called "the entry."

Most of the earlier Elliston houses had the kitchen placed at the front of the house, with the parlour (or bedroom) there also. The back of the house was usually taken up with a long entrance porch and a walk-in pantry or storeroom often referred to as the "linney" or "linnay." This storeroom might be half as big as the kitchen itself. Some families also had a separate outbuilding or "store" holding the winter's supply of flour, salt herring, turbot, beef, etc., especially if their pantry was small. Lots of space was needed for storing the winter food supply, much of which was bought "in bulk" when the head of the household "settled up" with the merchant each fall.

The porch, which occupied approximately half of the back section of the house, was a cold cheerless place in wintertime and little better in summer. Here the snow would be swept off outer garments and footwear, or muddy feet would be wiped clean in a rough mat (perhaps just a burlap sack), because no casual visitors ever removed their footwear before entering the kitchen, nor did they remove any other articles of clothing either. In early times the porch floor was just the "bare wood." Few housewives wasted a colourful hooked rug on this floor, except perhaps one which was practically worn out. The "gully" (water barrel) and the water buckets would be placed there both winter and summer. The family washtub, the washpan for the washing of face and hands, usually on its own stand, the pail for holding dirty water, the broom, and the scrubbing brush, each had a place here.


FURNISHINGS

The kitchen, the heart of the home, was undoubtedly the most comfortable room in the house and was the "living" room. Here was the cookstove which doubled as the heater for the home; so, in winter the kitchen was the only warm part of most houses. My informants assured me that the earliest stove in use in Elliston was the "Waterloo." Its cooking area with four removeable "tops" (stove lids) was supported on four legs and there was a longer leg at the back to support the oven. Because these stoves were rather low, they were often placed on a raised wooden area 2″–3″ high in the floor called the "hearth." The use of this name for the floor area concerned indicates its connection with the open fireplace which the cookstove replaced.

Another iron cookstove of later introduction, in common use in Elliston up till and after the 1940s, was the "Improved Standard." This stove differed from the Waterloo in that the oven was attached directly to the main stove instead of being separated from it by a neck. Both ovens though had doors at either end. Both stoves had a deep firebox in the front and a fender which could slide out when the ashes had to be taken out of the stove. There were small side doors in the firebox, too, so that fuel did not always have to be put in at the top. Behind the firebox and underneath the cooking area was a rectangular piece of iron which spanned the space between the firebox and the leg supporting the oven. Here was a quick drying area for mittens and socks. Wood for splits used to be dried out here, and it was also a convenient place to store the pressing irons. I remember seeing either a Waterloo or an Improved Standard in every kitchen I visited as a child. In our kitchen there was an Improved Standard manufactured in Amherst, Nova Scotia.

A still later introduction was the "coalburner." We had one of these in our dining room when I was a child. I remember it as being a rectangular, box-like stove on four legs, with the oven underneath the cooking area, unlike the Waterloo and Improved Standard which had theirs at the back. Its form was strange to those used to the Waterloo and one story I heard as a child was about a man in Elliston who bought a "coalburner." He spent all day looking for the oven, and the man who sold the stove to him pretended he could not find the oven either. The coalburner was similar in form to the wood-and-coal-burning ranges which preceded the oil-burning ranges in general use today; unlike them though it had two doors to the oven.

Stoves were modified over the years to suit the conditions. People used the kind of fuel available to them. Householders used wood in the early stoves and in the summertime all through the years the fuel for a quick fire was "blassy" boughs (dried fir branches) or dry spruce boughs. At one time during the thirties, some people burned peat in their stoves. By the 1940s coal was being widely used so the stove was fitted with coal-burning grates. The wood box, situated in the corner near the stove, was found in all kitchens. This the children of the family were expected to fill up daily, especially during the winter.

Several people told me that some early kitchens had a "planchen" (floor) covered with tar paper, except for about a foot around each side which was left bare. This border was kept clean by scrubbing with sand and soap, and quite often with a brush made from dried spruce boughs from which the needles had fallen. The "felt" was tarred once a year. Sometimes sand was sprinkled over it; but usually a "tarred" floor was polished with a mixture of tar and oil. "The smell got into your clothes, but you could see yourself in the floor," said William Crewe. More often the kitchen floor was left bare of covering but sand was sprinkled over it.

By the 1940s most houses in Elliston had some sort of "canvas" (cheap linoleum) on the kitchen floor. Usually this was a thin, felt-backed type, from which the enameled surface was soon scrubbed off and had to be replaced at least once a year. Some older homes had "Grand Falls" canvas. This was very thick, strong linoleum and was painted every year with a special floor enamel, the usual colours being dark green or dark brick red. The painting of such a floor caused a minor upheaval in our home when I was a child. For two or three days we had the delightful experience of "living" in the dining room until the floor dried properly. I have no idea how people with only one chimney or one cookstove managed this matter. Today, linoleum and tile floors are usual in the newer or renovated older homes.

In the early 1900s and through the 1940s, "hooked" rag mats were on all kitchen floors. These were in all manner of gay colours and designs and were placed around the floor according to the housewife's ideas of what was correct. I have a vague recollection of a big mat in front of the stove in our kitchen, but I don't know where the others were placed.

The kitchen was simply furnished, often with homemade pieces. A large table, frequently the type with two leaves which could be let down when the table was not in use, was usually located by one of the two windows. A long and wide "settle" or "couch" as it was sometimes called, was placed along one wall. The settle had a back and a covered "head" at one end. Sometimes the bench section was bare, but often it had a feather-filled cushion stretching the length of it, or else there were several smaller feather cushions scattered along its length.

Enough ordinary chairs for the family were placed around the room. These differed from house to house but there was a sameness about them. All were wooden with runged backs, and some were locally made. Most kitchens had a high-backed rocking chair. Many housewives also liked to have one or two "barrel chairs." These were made from a barrel with a section cut out, the remaining portion forming the back. A hinged seat was placed halfway up the barrel, so that there was a place for storage under the seat. Perhaps a bit of colourful cotton and a cushion might add to the comfort of the barrel-chair, but in poorer homes it stood naked except for paint. In addition to being comfortable seats, barrel-chairs were valuable storage areas for items used every day — mittens, "vamps" (the short, ankle-length socks worn over longer stockings), scarves, etc. Some housewives found barrel-chairs excellent storage places for the week's supply of potatoes on winter nights. Unless well covered, things could and did freeze inside the houses on frosty nights, as there was no fire on during the hours of sleeping.

Many homes had long benches or stools in the kitchen. These fitted into convenient corners under windows or shelves or in the chimney cor-

106

ner. At mealtimes they could be placed at the table to give seating for several persons.

Most kitchens had a "dresser" or "sideboard" which usually occupied the space between the chimney and the outer wall. Sometimes it was freestanding; other times it was a "built-in." The wide counterlike top was open and here most of the dishes were stored. Often there were higher, narrow shelves which held special, rarely used dishes, souvenirs, and "nicknacks," e.g., shells, china ornaments. In some homes the top section of shelves was enclosed by glass doors, especially if the cabinet were built into the wall. There was one like this in my aunt Beck's (Rebecca's) kitchen. The space underneath was closed also with two doors. It might be used for the storage of items for table use, or it might simply be a storage area for unmended clothes, or those which were in daily use. The cooking utensils, nearly all of iron or tin, were stored either in the closet under the stairs, or in the "linney."

The kitchen walls in every home were decorated with calendars supplied by the various businesses in the community. Dr. Chase's and Dodd's almanacs usually shared a nail or small hook in a corner. Often there was a small mirror and several pictures of varying types including the "Orange Chart" prominently displayed. This was a colourful chart depicting various Biblical events. Most members of the Loyal Orange Society possessed such a chart and its being on a wall indicated that some male in the family was an "Orangeman."

Nearly every home had a "mantel piece" in kitchen and parlour, the shelf, placed three-quarters up the wall above the stove. The woodwork for this was often intricately carved and difficult to dust. Here small ornaments and "treasures" were placed. In homes with small children, matches needed for lighting the fire were also placed here to be near at hand but out of reach of the children.

A few of the larger houses had a "back kitchen" for summer use only. The hurried housewife looked upon such a room as a time-saver for her regular kitchen could stay spick and span as the "dirty" work was confined to the summer kitchen. Some very "house proud" women even used an outside store, a shed, for summer cooking and eating; but the majority felt that kitchens were put in homes for use. "Show" was what the parlour was for.

Aunt Hilda said, "Our kitchen was also living and dining room." And a man remarked:

There's people had what they calls parlours then times never hardly went in 'um. That's the funny people. Build a house and have a room and never go in 'n."

His wife added:

> Perhaps it might be used at Christmas time or a birthday. Not very often a birthday cause probably have a little bit of birthday cake 'twouldn't be worth asking anybody to it, lots of times. But, Christmas, most commonly Christmas time, they'd have their little fire in there."

As may be seen from the above, the parlour or inside place was used very rarely. All entertaining was done in the kitchen except for very special occasions or when an important guest like the minister was present.

How people outside your immediate family furnished their "inside" rooms and "upstairs" was a deep mystery during the period 1900–1950. Rarely did any visitor get to see a neighbour's inside place. You might get an occasional glimpse of the hallway and the inside place through an open door, but you never ventured through that door no matter how great your curiosity. When you visited you got no further than the kitchen. There you sat down and did not wander around. Although the kitchen was public, in that you did not knock but walked right into the room, the rest of the house was very private. Only women who helped out in time of sickness or childbirth or "laying out" invaded the sanctity of the house beyond the kitchen.

In my description of "inside places" and "upstairs", therefore, I must rely mainly on what I knew personally as a child of my home and my close relatives' homes. This is supplemented with details learned from my various informants.

What parlours and other rooms were like and how they were furnished depended on the family's means and its size. A man with a big family to support on what a shareman could earn could not furnish his house in the style that the owner or part-owner of one or two cod-traps could. Most "inside places" seem to have had a "parlour stove," an upholstered sofa, some better quality chairs, perhaps an organ, and inevitably family portraits in heavy ornate frames. And in later years it might have "pretty flowerdy canvas" on the floor as well as hooked mats. Family members would be laid out in the parlour when they died. Perhaps this is why people avoided using these rooms. They were more "dead" than "living" rooms.

In the early days some of the better-off planters and the merchant's family had items imported from England. Luxury items like Grandfather clocks and musical instruments were brought from the Mother Country and they also imported furniture like dining tables, chairs, sofas, and desks as well. But the majority of the residents relied on their own skill or that of recognized local carpenters. In the early 1900s and during the forties as well, most of the furniture in the majority of homes was still locally made, but in this period those who wanted "better" furniture ordered it from St. John's through some company's agent.

By the 1900s most of the homes had four bedrooms upstairs. Much of the bedroom furniture, except that in the "best" or "spare" room (found in a few homes), had been locally made. Ordinarily bedrooms were furnished with a bed (usually a double one), a bureau with an attached mirror, and perhaps a smaller "washstand" (sometimes equipped with pitcher, bowl, and commode), a hard chair, and perhaps a trunk or chest for storage. Few bedrooms had built-in closets, and until moveable wardrobes became common, clothing was hung on hooks behind the bedroom doors, sometimes with dust cloths for protection. In the poorer homes there would be little furniture in most bedrooms except one or two beds.

The early homemade bedsteads were of wood which had a tightly knotted network of rope instead of springs to hold the bedding. By 1900 iron bedsteads, bought in the local stores and probably brought in from St. John's, had replaced most of these. Sometimes they had elaborate designs at the head and foot, and Aunt Hilda said that as a child she got great amusement out of the four brass knobs that were on the bedposts. "They could be screwed on and off." The first iron bedsteads were fitted with "laths." Three or four flat metal strips went lengthwise and fitted into protruding knobs at the top and foot of the bed. Five or seven went crosswise. The whole formed a web of metal on which the bedding rested. Later laths were replaced by springs. A heavy wooden frame with a network of wire was laid on the iron frame of the bedstead. Often an iron bar spanned the middle of the bedstead underneath the laths or the springs. Next a "bunk," a loose coarse mattress of wood shavings covered in flour sacking or "cotton duck", was placed on the laths or rope or wire netting. This protected the feather bed, which was encased in a special blue striped material called bed ticking. Everyone used feather beds in the early days, and they were very common during the 1940s.

109

Housewives used a set of flannelette sheets on each feather bed. These sheets were often homemade as flannelette material could be bought cheaply by the pound. Several cotton quilts were on every bed in most homes for all housewives believed that the weight of bedclothing was a guarantee of its warmth. Pillows in the old days were the big bolster feather-filled type which went "fore and aft" the bed. In addition, some adults used smaller feather pillows on top of the bolster, perhaps because they wanted more height. I suspect though that women encouraged their use in order to "save" the big pillow slip from becoming too stained, since men did not shampoo their hair very frequently, if at all, and oily stains were difficult to get out with ordinary washing.

During the 1940s mattresses were coming into general use, and these have now replaced the feather bed in most homes. Blankets replaced quilts somewhat later, but quilts have not totally disappeared from the scene. Today, in the majority of homes, housewives use small pillows filled with either feathers or foam rubber, but the bolster pillow is still used in some homes.

In the old days, no bed was properly "made" unless it had a "bed strip" or valance attached to the bed frame and going round the front and ends of the bed. This was a strip of white material, usually shirting, which was trimmed with handmade lace. It was a great dust catcher because it touched the floor, but it did hide whatever was under the bed — often a "johnny" pot (chamber pot). When they put away the bed strips, around the 1930s, some of the women said their beds looked awfully bare, for, although they had "counterpanes" for covering the top of the bed, they were not as long as the present day bedspreads and there might be a foot or more of space between the bed clothes and the floor.

In the old days the floors upstairs had no protective covering, but by the 1900s most people had some sort of thin "canvas" on their floors. Everyone, of course, had hooked rag mats, and some people had sheepskin or goatskin rugs, the latter being very common. When a goat was slaughtered in the fall, the man of the house would take the skin, scrape off any fat and work the hide. Then he would stretch it on a frame which he nailed onto an outbuilding until it had cured properly.

Walls, upstairs and down, were papered in the early 1900s, and the custom still persisted in the 1950s, though women did not need to paper as frequently then as formerly. Said Mrs. Orpah Crewe:

They looked real well too. Paper it spring and fall, see. You'd

110

paper it in the spring and then for Christmas you'd put a bit of paper on again. Paper wasn't so very dare [expensive] then. There was a lot of work to it though but [we] didn't mind the work."

There was indeed a lot of work to papering a room. The rolls were narrow, only seventeen to eighteen inches wide for the ordinary wall paper; the more expensive variety might be thirty inches wide. It was not pre-pasted. Housewives had to make their own paste, a mixture of flour and water, and this had to be the proper consistency so that the paper would stick well. Bare walls in a new house were first of all covered with "shadin'" (sheathing) paper. This was a sort of heavy construction paper about a yard wide, and usually cream-coloured. To insure this heavy paper stuck to the board, women often added lye to the paste, which meant they had to be extremely careful with the paste container and the paste itself; the mixture was poisonous and dangerous, especially for small children.

In rooms outside the "living" area, papering and painting would not have to be done every spring and fall; but every conscientious housewife would do her kitchen if she could afford it at all. For the walls would have become spotted with children's fingerprints, discoloured with smoke, and in summer the ever-present flies left their "fly spits" everywhere. Screen doors and window screens were unknown till the 1940s; some housewives in early years used thin muslin to screen upstairs windows and succeeded in keeping down the fly damage there. Downstairs though, in hot weather the back door stood wide open and the flies just poured inside. Sticky flypaper suspended from the kitchen ceiling was unsightly and not too effective and a fly swatter was a messy tool. So, people just lived with it. Several of my informants remarked wonderingly on how they ever managed to put up with having so many flies around.

At certain times there was a great deal of "paintin" and paperin'." Orpah Crewe described it this way:

> Get your bit of paper with the roses on it. The rosier the paper 'd be the better, you see. Some people liked striped paper. A stripe 'd go down the roses and some more wouldn't get that 'fraid their homes would'n't fair [i.e. plumb] and it'd be too much trouble to put that on, tryin' to get it fair. But with the roses all over it, the paper, if twas a little bit asquish [out of line], you wouldn't know it. [Roses meant any sort of floral design the wallpaper might have.]

111

Many housewives, of course, did have better surfaces to deal with than others, but the quality of the finished work depended on the women themselves. It is a fact that some women were much more capable paper hangers, took more pride in their work, and made sure their patterns matched perfectly every time, while others thought that all they had to do was cut and paste, and they never did master the art of papering a room properly.

In some houses the kitchen walls had the bottom part finished in "beaded" lumber. This was grooved three inch wide board which had a raised pattern on it and was the usual type used for ceilings. All ceilings, windows, and doors were painted. Kitchen ceilings were often light blue or a pale cream (buff). Window frames were often white or painted the same colour as the ceiling; door colours varied. Some householders painted them a solid colour — cream, blue, brown, or green; others liked to have the panels one colour and the frame a darker colour. A door in one house was jokingly referred to as "blood blue"! One elderly couple told me that doors might have white panels and be painted yellow or brown "out around." Since it was only in exceptional cases that one went past the kitchen in a neighbour's house, I cannot say how rooms beyond the kitchen were painted and none of my informants mentioned this. In our house white paint was used on all woodwork — the stairs, ceilings, window frames, thresholds, "skirting" (baseboards), except in the kitchen and porch. There it was more practical to have a slightly darker colour.

### HOUSEKEEPING

None of the early homes had running water. There were only one or two homes that boasted this convenience even during the thirties and forties. In fact there were very few private wells in Elliston Centre until comparatively recent times. Most people got their water supply from the various brooks flowing through their community and which were deepened in spots, forming "wells." People in Maberly were better provided with water than were their neighbours on the Neck, just half a mile away. For years there were two or three private wells in the former section of the community, and two public wells. On the Neck there was but one shallow public well which went dry nearly every summer. Then the inhabitants were faced with the task of bringing water from Maberly or from the running brook at Sandy Cove, which like Maberly was a half mile away though in the opposite direction.

Most homes kept their daily water supply in a "gully" (water barrel) placed in the back porch. It was a common sight in summertime to see five or six women or older girls heading for a well with hoops (circular or square wooden frames which rested on the rims of the buckets and kept the buckets from hitting the person's legs) and buckets on their arms. They would carry home about five gallons of water each at a time and would need to make five or six trips to fill the gully.

Most homes, especially if they were situated a considerable distance from the sea, had outdoor toilets or "privies." Other people had pits, some distance from the house, on which they also threw their daily buckets of wood ashes. Many housewives simply emptied their "slop pails" over a nearby cliff into the sea. This emptying of pails was a chore that had to be done early in the morning so people, especially the men, would not see it being done. Dishwater and wash or scrub water was simply thrown into the backyard. There might or might not be a drain to carry this away. Male members of the family rarely made use of inside facilities (pail or chamber pot) except perhaps in the wintertime. Their toilet was the "trunkhole," in the stage. This was a hole about one and half feet sqaure in the floor through which a bucket was lowered to bring up sea water.

Before electricity came to the main part of the community in the 1920s, other daily household jobs included the trimming and cleaning of lamps. There was usually a large one used in the kitchen and at least one small one for upstairs use. If there was only one "upstairs" lamp, it might be left burning in one of the children's bedrooms until the parents took it to their room when they retired. The lamp stand, as the base was called, and the part which held the kerosene were usually of glass, although some lamps had iron stands. The kitchen lamp was often mounted on a wall in an iron bracket with a reflector behind it to direct the light on any special area where a better light was needed. In some kitchens the lamp was placed on the kitchen table at night, and on a corner shelf in the kitchen during the day. Each day the kerosene supply had to be replenished, the chimney or lamp "globe" had to be polished, and the wick had to be trimmed so that the flame burnt evenly with no "snookers" (the little jibs of flame which smoked up the lamp chimney).

In summertime if there was much nightwork in the stage, the women had to see that the "stage lamps" and lanterns were trimmed as well. These stage lamps were simply tin kettles holding perhaps a pint of kerosene. There were two spouts through which the wicks were pulled. The flames from the wicks were not covered and the light given off was a reddish-yellow glow. There was a handle attached to the rim so that the lamp could be suspended above the working area by means of a wire.

Although many homes were provided with electricity in the 1920s, electricity was used only for lighting. There were very few appliances used until after the second World War. And because housewives during this period lacked the many conveniences which modern housewives in the community deem essential, they had to put in long hours at chores which have disappeared today.

Before a housewife could even begin a major chore like the weekly wash, she had to make proper preparations. First of all, she had to make sure she had lots of water on hand, and she might have to bring this from a distance of half a mile or more. The water had to be heated in containers, usually iron pots or kettles in the old days, on the stove. Badly soiled garments would be put in a boiler along with some wood ashes tied up in a bag and the clothes boiled until the dirt "boiled out" of them. But the greater part of the family wash, underwear for the different family members, the men's and boys' best shirts, men's workshirts, girls' and women's work dresses or blouses, aprons, handkerchiefs, sheets and pillow cases, were washed by hand. Washing was done either in the kitchen, or in the porch, more often in the latter when the weather was not too cold.

Wooden washtubs were being used by the majority of housewives even in the 1940s. "You were high up if you had a galvanized tub and a scrubbing board," said Jane Pearce. Great care had to be taken of these wooden tubs both winter and summer. In summer water had to be kept in them continually so that they would not split and fall apart in the heat; in winter they had to be kept inside the house lest the frost "draw them apart." Usually these tubs were fashioned from the bottom of a flour barrel, with two portions protruding for handles, or else two hand holes were cut just below the rim. By the 1940s most women were using scrub boards, either an all wooden type with a ribbed surface for scrubbing on, or else one with a wooden frame and ribbed glass. Some women would not use scrubbing boards at all. My mother did not. She contended that rubbing on the boards was hard on clothes, so she used only hands and knuckles for eradicating stubborn spots.

Most women would consider it a disgrace to hang out a dirty, dingy wash. Those who advertise detergents on television today are working on this folk feeling; but women in my grandmother's day achieved the desired result without commercial bleaches or detergents. Women in Elliston had to make their own washing agents in the old days and each fall made a product called "blubber" soap or "soft" soap. "Blubber" (rotten cod livers) and wood ashes were boiled in a pot until stringy like "lassy candy." The reason for the name blubber soap is obvious; it was called "soft" soap because, although they cut it into bars after it cooled, it never really hardened properly.

In the thirties and forties, housewives no longer made blubber soap. For washing and scrubbing they used either Bibby or Sunlight soap, whichever was available in the Elliston shops. To make this bought soap go farther, housewives cut the long bars into short pieces, placed them in a paper bag and hung them up beside the chimney to harden. In the forties badly soiled clothing was still boiled in an iron pot on the stove in a lye solution, but instead of wood lye women used a commercial product, Gillet's Lye. This lye was stronger than wood lye and had to be treated with care. Clothes boiled in lye were lifted out of the pot very gingerly with a long stick and then plunged into tubs of cold water. Clothes got several rinses before they were deemed safe enough to be handled with the bare hands. I remember Mother doing this rinsing out in the yard, not in the porch where she usually did the washing; for lots of water got slopped around. Blueing was always added in the final rinse for white things.

Many delicate items that just needed a little bleaching would be spread out on the grass while still damp for the sun to act on for a day or so. These items were then rinsed and hung on the line to dry properly. Women always preferred to dry clothing outside, if at all possible, even in freezing weather. Many women felt that clothes dried in the house dried "drenty" (not a bright clean white). Few people in the old days had long clotheslines; twenty feet was the usual length. The "best things," like sheets and pillowcases and delicate items, would be dried on the line in the yard, but heavier things would be put on the fence.

Monday was the washday for most housewives, though some like my mother, were not tied to any particular day, but chose the first suitable one for the weekly washing. In winter a woman might be able to stick to a fairly rigid schedule and get her washing done on Monday; but in summer if the fish were plentiful, her schedule was altered to fit the conditions. As Orpah Crew put it:

You might put your clothes in soak, but that's as far as you'd get sometimes. Perhaps they'd have to lie in water for a couple of days before you got around to it. The water'd go sour on you."

Aunt Hilda commented also:

The wash might be in soak all Monday if a lot of fish. Otherwise it would be finished on Monday. First the wash was put on the grass or low trees to bleach and then on Wednesday it was taken up and rinsed over. Blueing and starch were put in at the second washing. Really, washing and ironing was a week's work.

My informants on the Neck told me that sometimes during a dry summer they would wash their clothes in the pond over at Sandy Cove, and would rinse them in warm water when they got back home.

Much starch was used in the early 1900s. At that time men favoured heavily-starched shirt fronts, and the white apron, which every married woman put on after finishing up her dirtier household chores, was also heavily starched. Most housewives used store-bought starch, though sometimes they used to make their own "flour starch." This was made very like the thickening for gravy, simply flour mixed with a large amount of water. In earlier days, around the 1840s, Elliston housewives used starch made from potatoes. Philip Tocque gives a full description of this "potato starch" in his book *Wandering Thoughts*:

Most of the inhabitants of Bird Island Cove [Elliston] make their own starch from the potatoes. A quarter of a bushel will make a pound; the process is very simple. The potatoes are just peeled, then grated over a tub of water, into which the potato falls. When a sufficient quantity is grated, it is well stirred about the tub with the hand; it is then taken and strained through a piece of fine calico or muslin, and let remain in a dish for a day, after which the starch is found in a thick, white coat on the bottom of the dish, and the water floating on top; the water is then thrown off, and the starch taken and put in a small bag and hung to dry.[1]

Most of my informants can remember when ironing was done with a "box iron." This was wedge-shaped and hollow. Special heaters were placed in the fire till they got red-hot. Then, by means of tongs, they were placed in the hollow of the box iron, and the shutter, which could be lifted up and down, was closed. There were generally two heaters with the box iron; while one was being used the other was getting hot.[2]

Another early iron was the "flat iron" which was heated on top of the stove. This was wedge shaped, in one piece handle and all; so it had to be removed from the stove with great care using something to protect oneself

116

from the hot handle. On the next type of iron, the "sad iron," the wooden handle was separate. Only the irons got heated on the top of the stove. The handle which lifted them off the stove fastened into the hole at the top of each iron and stayed cool for use. Sad irons came in a set of three of different weights and were pointed at both ends. My mother used sad irons. Many housewives did their ironing while they were baking bread, which could be any day of the week except Sunday. Then the stove was extremely hot and the irons heated up quickly. In summertime this was like ironing in an inferno, but both baking and ironing went on all through the year.

Women also had to keep up with their mending and darning at all seasons unless they wanted their children to be referred to as "rag molls" (children whose clothes were often getting torn and were left in that condition, unmended). In summer, of course, mending was often done hurriedly. Outside chores had priority. Lucky indeed was the housewife whose mother, mother-in-law, or other elderly relative, would help with the family mending. Apparently this often did happen for according to Aunt Hilda:

> Old women always did mending, knitting, making quilts. Took a lot of work off the young wife.

Other weekly household chores besides ironing might be done any day of the week, but "Scrub-Day" was synonymous with Saturday, winter and summer, at least till the 1940s. In summer, a "good" housewife would have to rise very early on scrub-day if she wanted to get her work done before being involved with outside chores connected with the fishery. Of course if she employed a maid, or had a daughter old enough to do the work, it would be different. Even in winter most housewives tried to finish their scrubbing in the morning.

Scrub-Day followed a definite, almost ritualistic pattern. First the iron cook stove in the kitchen had to be "cleaned." Ashes were removed every day, but "cleaning" meant polishing. Early in the century, stove-lead or "blackening" was used. This was smeared on with a rag and polished with a brush. After the polishing "you had to be able to see your face in it," said Aunt Hilda, for a well-polished stove was one of the recognized marks of a good housewife.

Because this stove polishing sent black specks of polish everywhere, and because flies were not careful where they left their marks, it followed that nearly every surface except the ceiling and the papered walls, had to be washed. All the "paintwork" on the mantel piece, the windows, the doors, the skirting boards and the furniture was first washed with soap and water — carbolic or blubber soap in the old days and Sunlight or Bibby soap later on. Chairs were nearly always painted every year, but after a few scrubbings they lost their protective coating. William Crewe's earliest memory of an old neighbour woman was the whiteness of her well-scrubbed kitchen chairs.

After the paintwork, the floors in the kitchen and porch were cleaned. If it were "canvas-covered," a simple washing with soap and water would be sufficient. If it were "bare floor," it had to be scrubbed with a brush as well as being washed. Thresholds, as I mentioned earlier, got special treatment; they were scrubbed with a "fresh drop of water" so that they did not acquire a dirty grey cast after the paint wore off.

A major "job" was scrubbing the wooden bridge which led to the backdoor of every house. This got extremely dirty in muddy weather and had to be scrubbed frequently. Those few who had concrete steps were saved from much of this.

Friday was generally the day for cleaning the upstairs. Here dust was the chief enemy, so windows, doors, and furniture required only a light touch-up. Floors were washed, as were the stairs, which being usually painted white, had to be given special attention. The "inside place," which was little used, would only need a thorough cleaning every two weeks, though a light dusting would be in order in between times.

Certain household tasks only needed to be done once a year, but they were major chores. The greatest washing test of all faced the housewife every spring. In late May or early June, all the heavy winter quilts had to be washed and stored till they were needed again in the fall. Wringing the water out of these thick quilts was a gigantic task, but some women could perform this chore magnificently. Since quilts were usually too heavy to hang on the clothes line, they were spread over the fence in the backyard with ends pinned together with clothes pegs so they would not blow away when they got drier. Summer quilts were washed in the fall, but there were fewer of them and they were of lighter weight, hence the task was easier.

Every spring the whole house was turned "topsy turvy" for the semi-annual cleaning. People wanted to get rid of the grime of winter and freshen up the place for the summer. Every housewife who could afford it was busy with paper and paint. Even those who could not spend money were busy. On a bright sunny day in May or early June, all the "beds and bunks" and hooked mats were brought outside and aired for the full day. Feather "beds" and "shaving bunks" were punched and pummelled every which way to get rid of winter dust and dirt.

Mats and any other rugs were swept and beaten free of dust every Friday, but during spring cleaning the hooked mats got their annual scrubbing. Those who lived near a brook with a wooden bridge over it, found this an ideal spot for "scrubbing-out" their mats. They would arrive at the bridge with perhaps a dozen or more hooked rag mats. The mat would be spread out on the bridge and the woman or girl, standing perhaps on a stone in the brook, would slosh water over the mat and then work up a lather with some soap and scrub vigorously. When one side had been scrubbed to her satisfaction, she turned the mat over and did the same to the other side. When all the mats were scrubbed, they were taken to the sea and dunked in the salt water. This set the colours so that they wouldn't run, and also got rid of any soapy film. The dripping mats were then taken to the fish flake and laid on the wooden "longers" to dry in the sun. In two or three days they were ready for use once more. Some people also scrubbed their mats in the fall, but the majority of housewives were content with a spring cleaning for upstairs mats. Downstairs, where the mats got dirty fairly quickly, they might be scrubbed whenever the opportunity arose.

### FEEDING THE FAMILY

Although a woman had to spend a great deal of her time in keeping her family clean, this does not mean that she neglected to feed them. Much of a woman's time indoors was spent in the preparing and serving of food. Seeing the family were fed at the proper times was one task there was no getting away from or putting off till later. Even a woman who was not a good cook had to get meals ready. The content and number of meals, and how they were served, differed according to the season and the woman's workload outside the house.

No one, however, had less than four meals a day in winter and nearly twice as many in summer, unless he went to bed very early in the evening. The four meals — breakfast, dinner, tea, and a "mug-up" or "lunch" before bedtime — were standard in most homes during the winter. Meals might be eaten in a more leisurely fashion then and women could spend more time preparing them. In winter the housewife had a greater variety of foodstuffs to use. Supplies purchased in "bulk" in the fall consisted of:

beef and pork in barrels, flour in barrels or sacks, sugar in a sack, "butter" (margarine) in tubs or cartons, plus salted herring and salted turbot in barrels, which were stored in the linney or pantry or in an outside storage shed. In the storage shed also, was fresh meat or pork from an animal killed after the weather turned frosty. On the pantry shelves were bottles of homemade partridge berry, blueberry, and bakeapple jams. In the root cellar were homegrown vegetables. If the man of the house were a "gunner," there would be salt water birds for the table from time to time. Dinner at noon was always a big meal, winter or summer, but tea or "supper" in winter was also substantial, consisting perhaps of baked beans, or potato scallop, or boiled cod.

In summer, especially if fish were plentiful giving a busy trapping season, there would often be seven meals — the men's light snack in the early morning, breakfast around 7:30–8:00 a.m., mug-up at 10:30–11:00 a.m., dinner at 12:30–1:00 p.m., mug-up at 3:30–4:00 p.m., tea at 5:30–6:00 p.m., and a mug-up before bedtime at 10:30–11:00 p.m. or earlier.

Summer meals on weekdays were prepared, served, and eaten in as short a time as possible. They were generally less substantial than winter meals. By the end of the winter large families would have used up much of their bought supplies and their supplies of carrots, turnips, and cabbages. Even the basic vegetable, the potato, might be in short supply. People spoke of the "long hungry month of March," probably with good reason. Till the railroad came, people of the area were dependent on supplies brought in by ship to Bonavista or Catalina and carted from there. Often in summer there would not be much to "bring round a meal" except fish and bread.

Since no meal was complete without bread, it deserves special treatment. So before discussing standard meals I will talk about bread making, a daily task. Baking, that is, bread baking, was done every day, sometimes twice a day for large families. Bread was indeed the "staff of life." In some homes, bread and butter and tea might be eaten at every meal except dinner, and if vegetables were scarce, it might be eaten at that meal also. One cogent expression I heard in my childhood showed how one young boy from a large, not very well-off, family felt about such fare. Asked by an older brother what there was for supper, he replied: "nuttin' but 'chaw and glutch'!" Questioning revealed that supper was only of the bread and tea variety, which he found unappetizing and difficult to swallow.

In the old days women in the community used hops in bread making, and many of my informants can remember when hops were grown in some backyards. My mother often spoke of the hops which Aunt Helen Pearce grew in Maberly. However those women with whom I talked, used store-bought yeast when they first started making bread back in the early 1900s. The brands that were popular in the forties were Lallemands' and Royal. The former was sold in round, one-ounce slices, five or six in a cardboard container. Royal yeast was in square, one-ounce blocks, again with five or six in a container. Yeast cakes were kept covered in their containers in the pantry. The yeast cakes had to be soaked apart in lukewarm water with sugar; a small amount of flour was then added and mixed to a pasty consistency. This "barm," or sponge, was left to rise in some container in a warm place. Often a tin, three-quart, "boat's kettle" (a high, narrow pot with a tightly fitting cover and a hanger so the mixture might be suspended from a hook over the warm stove), was used. When this barm had risen sufficiently, it was added to about a half-gallon of water and sufficient flour in the "mixing pan." Few women used shortening, or butter, in the old days, and the salt added was often the coarse fishery salt. During the depression days of the thirties, women, if they had lots of potatoes, would boil some of these, mash them up and add this to the flour mixture to "make the flour go farther." I was told that potato "grounds" were also used for leavening when the housewife was short of regular yeast, but I do not know just what this was like.

Women used to bread making could mix up a batch in ten to fifteen minutes. But of course the finished product was not ready for eating till hours later. It took several hours to rise, then the dough was kneaded down and let rise again. Finally it was "put in the pans" and let rise again before it was put in the oven for baking, which took about one hour. Many women preferred to make their bread at night, especially in the summertime. Then it would rise during the night and baking could be done before the "heat of the day." In summer the kitchen at bread-baking time was extremely hot, with every bit of furniture nearly as hot as the stove itself.

Orpah Crew, mother of ten children, certainly mixed a lot of bread. She "made up" one and a half barrels of flour during one month in the spring when they ran out of potatoes early in the season. She would make the bread at night and bake it next morning. She said that often there would have to be two mixings a day. Then she might pinch off a small bit of dough and use this "leaven" for the second batch. "Had to be careful because bread could easily go sour when you used 'leaven'."

Housewives, when at all possible, tried to "bake ahead." No woman liked to cut freshly-baked bread. It was difficult to cut properly and you wasted a lot. No matter how a child longed for a slice of freshly-baked bread, mothers were adamant: "No cutting the hot bread!" My mother, if she were short of bread, satisfied our craving for hot bread by baking "buns off the bread." That is, she would take a portion of her bread dough, make small buns (rolls) and put them on a cookie sheet or other shallow pan to bake up quickly. These buns were nearly always eaten while still hot and the regular batch of bread was saved until it got cool.

Some families that were very badly off, perhaps with no mother to look after them, or one who was a poor cook, might even have to make do with "nochers" or "damper devils." This was chiefly flour and water mixed to a dough consistency, formed into a flat cake, and cooked on the top of a hot stove without benefit of a cooking utensil. Most women considered this poor fare indeed. Fortunately, those who had to go without proper bread were few, for the knowledge of bread making was one skill which all marriageable girls were expected to possess, and this was emphasized again and again by my women informants.

Today's cooks use instant yeast for bread making, and many still make their own bread in Elliston, although bakery products are available. Most of the menfolk refer to "baker's bread" as "baker's fog." They prefer the more substantial homemade variety.

The men's early morning snack during the fishing season was a light meal, usually bread and butter with tea. Perhaps they had a little jam or marmalade to "tow the bread down." The woman would set the table before she retired for the night and would lay a white cloth over everything to keep out the flies. The man would boil his own kettle and make his own tea for this early meal. This was the only indoor chore most men performed; but men always cooked their own meals on the fishing grounds and some were known to be "good cooks."

Women took care of all other meals. The regular breakfast eaten around 7:30–8:00 a.m. in the summer was often fresh codfish, either hot or cold. The bread was sliced and placed on a special bread plate. If anyone wanted toast, the bread would be laid on the cooking surface of the red hot stove or put in the hot oven. Since housewives usually made just a quick bough fire to boil the kettle and allowed it to go out afterward, toast was not as common on the summer breakfast table as it was in winter when the stove was always red hot and the oven could brown the sliced bread to a crisp very quickly. There were very few electric toasters in use until recent years.

Aunt Hilda told me that in the early 1900s oatmeal porridge was often served for breakfast in her house. They sweetened it with molasses and put a dab of butter on it as well. Sometimes a little milk was added. Fresh milk was used if available, but more often in winter they used tinned milk or none at all. During my childhood porridge was made from rolled oats. Sometimes for hot cereal we had cream of wheat or corn meal instead of rolled oats. We used sugar for sweetening instead of molasses. Dry cereals came to the breakfast table much later, probably only after World War II. Tea was drunk at every meal except perhaps dinner. Many older people remembered molasses as the chief sweetener for tea, but gradually sugar replaced it. In my childhood molasses was used for pudding sauces, in baking, and on children's after-school slices of bread (lassy-bread).

Eggs were not commonly eaten for weekday breakfasts, but only for Sunday breakfasts; and not even then when eggs were scarce as they often were during the winter. Though housewives tried to keep a stock of eggs, preserved in salt or flour, for their winter baking, they could not spare any for breakfast. Even in the forties eggs were still very scarce in winter. In fact breakfasts, winter and summer, had not altered very much from what they were in the early 1900s.

The mug-up, taken several times a day in summer, was a light meal — always bread and butter and tea and anything that was available for a "relish." In the early days this might be leftover fish or some homemade jam; in later years, cold meats, tinned beans, or jam. The mug-up before bedtime was a must in the majority of homes winter and summer, but it was usually just something light.

Dinner, the most substantial meal of the day, was served around midday. During weekdays in summer, it consisted chiefly of potatoes and codfish. Potatoes, either peeled or partly peeled (chipped), were always boiled. Since women were always making dinner in a hurry they often did not take time to peel the potatoes completely. They "chipped" the peel off around the "eyes" of the potato and other rough spots and boiled the potatoes in their holey jackets. Some people finished the peeling at the table, but others ate the potatoes, peels and all.

The fish might be cooked in a number of different ways. If the backbone were left in it, the housewife would either stew or boil it. A "stewed" fish was placed in a small amount of water in a pot on the stove. Onion slices and small cubes of salt beef were added to the water and fish. It would be ready for eating in half to three quarters of an hour. Boiled fish was simply and quickly cooked. The fish was placed in a little salted water and boiled in a pot. After it had boiled, it was strained and chives were mixed with it for flavouring. Salt pork would be cut into small cubes and fried out — the grease and the pork (scruncheons) were then poured over the fish.

If the cod was to be fried, first it was split, that is the backbone was removed. Then it was cut into suitable pieces, rolled in flour and placed in hot pork fat in the frying pan. No matter how the housewife cooked her daily fish, it never took up much time, usually half to three quarters of an hour before a substantial meal was ready for serving.

Fish for the noon meal in summer was obtained daily. A woman whose husband was fishing would either get it from the stage herself, or have someone in the family get one for her. But if a woman happened to have no one fishing, she would then have to send one of her children along to someone's stage while they were "putting away the fish." Rarely did the child ask for a fish. He or she simply stood there until some member of the crew asked if he wanted a fish. When he said "yes," or nodded in reply, he would then be asked: "Does your mother want to fry it?" If the answer was again, "Yes," they would remove the backbone. If "No," they would just take off the head and "insides" before giving it to the child. Salmon was a delicacy which most families might have four or five times during the summer when they happened to be caught in the cod-trap. Like cod, it was either boiled or fried.

There were no fresh fish of any kind eaten during the winter, but fish was still served once or twice a week. There were salted herring and turbot, kept in pickle, as well as cured salted cod. Salt beef formed the core of most winter dinners and in the earlier days "Hambutt" pork was also cooked for a bit of variety. Hambutt pork differed from "fat-back" pork used for frying purposes in that "it had a bone in it."

Soup, that is vegetable soup, was a common dinner meal when there were plenty of homegrown vegetables available. It might be made with either fresh or salt meat, and usually contained carrots, turnips, parsnips, and potatoes cut into small pieces. Women always thickened this vegetable soup with rice, which is why they often referred to it as rice soup. Sometimes dumplings were added as an extra. Pea soup was a common Saturday meal in many homes. We never had pea soup in our house, however, because father disliked peas. Both rice and pea soup were very thick soups.

In late fall, most families could enjoy fresh meat or fresh pork at din-

124

nertime for a little while, if they slaughtered a cow, or goat, or sheep, or pig. The carcass was hung from a beam in some outbuilding while the weather was cold. But if there were a large amount, it would have to be salted down in order to keep it any length of time. There were no professional butchers in Elliston. A man would do the slaughtering himself, perhaps with help from a neighbour. Carcasses were cut up with no regard for special cuts.

In the 1940s, sea birds were quite plentiful in the Elliston area. Men often went "gunning" especially during the fall and winter months. My father and those who "gunned" with him went after eider or hound ducks. Turrs were not part of our winter diet as they were not common in our area. As a child, I remember references to "old" turrs. The only ones we saw were cripples that had drifted to the shore. "Bawks" ("eggdowns" or shearwaters) were often killed during the summer months. During foggy weather these birds used to come very close to the fishing boats after the bait on the trawls. So these fishermen had more opportunity to get bawks than trapmen. When a bawk alighted on the water near the boat, someone in the boat "batted" (hit) it over the head with the "bawk pole," which all fishermen carried in their boats. Two local men one day killed some bawks and tossed them in the bottom of the boat with "gangboards" covering them. When they returned from the fishing grounds they threw the bawks up on the stagehead. To their consternation two or three of the "dead" birds flew away. Of course, these birds had been stunned by the blow from the bawk pole, not killed, and had revived on the way to shore. Sea birds meant a nice change in the menu and if more birds were killed than could be used up, these were salted down for later use.

With every "cooked" meal, i.e., dinner, in winter, there were always potatoes, plus two or more vegetables, namely turnips, cabbages, carrots, parsnips or beets. In summer, when most root cellars were almost empty, people considered themselves lucky even to have enough potatoes to cook. If these were used up it meant there had to be much more bread baked, perhaps two mixings a day.

Tea, served around 5:30–6:00 p.m., was more substantial than a mug-up, but less substantial than dinner. Since most housewives cooked more than enough vegetables for dinner, there were always leftovers. These vegetables were usually all mashed together, perhaps with onion added, and heated up in a frying pan, for the main supper dish, "hash." Any leftover meat or fish would be eaten with the hash or there might be some tinned meat or bologna. Often though, the housewife would serve

125

something made especially for supper, for example, baked beans. It depended on the season of the year.

Women set the table in the same way for every meal but dinner. Usually a tablecloth made from flour sacking, or some cheap cotton material for weekdays, was laid over the oilcloth-covered kitchen table. At every place was put a cup and saucer, a tea plate, a knife, and sometimes a fork. Teaspoons were placed in a glass spoon holder on the table. Butter was in a covered butter dish, and most housewives liked to have pretty covers for their butter dishes. Sugar, when used, was in a covered sugar basin (bowl), often with a special sugar "shell" (spoon). Molasses, used in the old days, was put in a special molasses bowl with a cover. Milk was served in a small jug (pitcher). Bread was piled high on a special bread plate and was on the table for every meal except dinner. If jam was being eaten, there might be a special "jam dish" at each place, if not you used your tea plate. For dinner, bigger "dinner" plates replaced tea plates and water glasses were laid instead of tea cups. If soup were the main course, soup plates or bowls would be used and soup spoons. Rarely did people have a cup of tea after the main course on week-days.

On Sunday the table was spread with the best tablecloth of linen or good quality cotton. Sunday meals, all through the year, differed from weekday meals and were as special as the larder could afford. Since in the early 1900s no unnecessary work was done on Sunday, Sunday's meals had to be prepared on Saturday, i.e., the vegetables cleaned. Some older women do this even today. So strictly was the rule adhered to in the early days that if unexpected company turned up for Sunday dinner in some households, the visitors would have to make do with what was already prepared. Miss Lily Pearce said: "I don't know if Father'd [even] go to the cellar to get anything else."

A favourite Sunday breakfast, winter and summer, was "fish and brewis." In summer the fish would be fresh; in winter it would be cured. Brewis was made by soaking hardtack or "hard bread" (sea biscuit) overnight in cold water till the hard cakes were softened. This was brought to a boil but not allowed to boil. "Grease and scruncheons" (hot fat and small fried cubes of salt pork) was poured over the softened hard bread. Sometimes the fish and the brewis (pronounced "brews") were served in separate portions; on other occasions the fish and the brewis were mixed together before serving, called "fisherman's brewis". Lily Pearce was very emphatic about the difference. Said she:

Not fish and brewis. We used to have 'fisherman's brewis.' All put together. Fish cooked in one pot, brewis in another, that's fresh fish now. And then when it cooked all put together with hot fat and scruncheons, we call it, and onion. And we'd have that on Sunday morning for breakfast. Everybody up Sunday morning for breakfast. And the next Sunday morning, instead of fisherman's brewis, it would be eggs. Everybody had plenty of hens. And . . . you had to listen to father readin' the Bible after breakfast. No getting out.

Sunday dinner was always the best dinner of the week. Even if there were no "fresh meat" or chicken, and frequently before the days of refrigeration there was none, there would be an extra lot of salt beef and plenty of vegetables — potatoes, parsnips, turnips, cabbages, carrots, and beets. Sometimes in late spring and summer if supplies of most homegrown vegetables had run out, people cooked dry beans and peas which could be bought in the local stores. The "pease" pudding was cooked in a small bag in the pot with the other vegetables.

A pudding always "finished off" the Sunday dinner. This was usually a "boiled pudding" or "figgy" pudding, containing soaked bread, flour, spices and raisins. Over this pudding most women used "cody" (sauce). Said Lily Pearce:

> My mother used to make it with sugar, butter, water and vinegar. She'd cook it until it got thick. That was the cody she used to make . . . I make cody now, on times. And I make it with milk and sugar, a little water, vanilla and cornstarch.

Other possibilities were vinegar and sugar mixed on the plate. In early days molasses was frequently used.

Sunday tea was a lighter meal than the dinner at midday, but it was a substantial meal. Most housewives liked to have two courses on Sunday. In winter, salt codfish, watered carefully, i.e., soaked overnight, and then boiled, was the main course, along with homemade bread. During the summer, a "scrod" was often Sunday night supper. "Scrod" was the name given a cod prepared in a special way. It was sprinkled with a little salt and left overnight. In the morning, it was washed and dried and perhaps hung on the line to cure slightly in the sun. When it was ready for cooking, it was put in a pan in the oven with salt pork over it and cooked in a moderate oven for three-quarters to one hour. It was eaten with bread.

For the second course, people might have custard or jam, or in later years, "jelly" (a gelatine dessert) and "blancmange" (made with cornstarch and milk). Usually too there was raisin bread, and many people tried to have "sweet cake" (layer cake, jam tart, etc.) to provide a finish to the meal along with a cup of tea.

Sunday meals were special all through the year, but the most special meals of all were served at Christmas; no matter on which day of the week it fell. The Christmas Eve supper was very much like the usual Sunday supper: people tried to have "watered fish," i.e., salt cod, and the sweet treat at this meal was raisin bread.

The Christmas breakfast was nothing very special, particularly since children would have little appetite for food. They would have gorged themselves on apples, oranges, grapes and candy from their Christmas stockings — goodies rarely seen during the rest of the year — for in the early 1900s and during the Depression days of the thirties, they were luxuries. In fact once during the thirties my brother Clifford, then three or four years old, found green grapes in his stocking on Christmas morning. He had never seen green grapes before and, at first, refused to eat them, saying: "Santa Claus put 'pratie buds' in my stocking."

From 1900 through the 1940s, fresh local meat or pork (your own or someone else's) was the main course on the Christmas dinner table. Turkey has become the main dish only within recent years, after World War II and refrigeration. Vegetables and dessert were the same as those for an ordinary Sunday dinner. Perhaps the pudding might contain a few more raisins, and there would be "suet" (fat from a goat or cow) included with the spices, flour, bread and molasses.

Christmas tea or supper might feature some of the leftovers from dinner for the main course, but for the second course the table was crowded with as many kinds of "sweet cake" as the housewife had in the house. Certainly "the Christmas Cake" was always cut at this time. This cutting of the Christmas cake was the high point of the meal in most families.

The Christmas cake in most homes was a rich, dark fruit cake, but there were as many different recipes followed as there were housewives, and much variation in quality and taste. In fact, some women over the years built up reputations for making delicious Christmas cakes. In grandmother's day, none of the women in Elliston had cookbooks and few followed written recipes. In the old days they did not have "prepared" fruit, but some managed to get citron and lemon peel for their Christmas Cake. This was bought in long strips and it was the job of the young girls to cut

128

it into small pieces. Said Aunt Hilda. "the flavour seemed nicer then, than now." They used raisins too, but the big seeded kind had to have the seeds removed. Currants were in common use, but housewives rarely used nuts in their baking until the 1920s.

In mother's day cookbooks were becoming more common in the kitchen, and women also tried out recipes given on the "Homemaker's Page" in the *Family Herald*, a weekly farming newspaper found in a great many Elliston homes.

Housewives in the thirties and forties, if they could afford it, obtained the same candied fruits as are available today. Cherries, lemon, citron, and orange peels, raisins, seeded and unseeded, currants, dates and walnuts were widely used. Both in the early 1900s and later, housewives used a variety of spices along with molasses, flour, eggs and butter. Most women used the artificial lemon or vanilla flavourings, but others used a small drop of wine, or even rum.

Other Christmas delicacies might include a light fruit cake, several plain "layer cakes" with jam between the layers, a light loaf cake with raisins, "patties" (small bun cookies), raisin bread, and "barksail" bread (molasses flavoured bread with no raisins). Housewives in recent years, have added chocolate cakes and a bewildering array of cookies. Even today, most housewives try to have plenty of fancy baked goods on hand for the entire Christmas season.

For many people, especially those with very large families in the old days, and for most families during the Depression, "sweet cake" was a luxury; there was only sufficient at special occasions like Christmas. Most women, unless they were extremely poor, did "Christmas baking" and tried to bake enough goodies to last for the twelve days of Christmas, for anyone might drop in during that period. In the old days "some people tried to get a slice of Christmas cake from twelve different houses to ensure twelve months of happiness,"[3] said Mary Jane Porter. No visitor could leave the house without a "bit of Christmas" — a sampling of the Christmas cake, plus other lesser kinds, and a drink. The drink might be tea or hot peppermint, or even cold syrup during recent years. Few women took anything stronger, though some would sample the home-brewed wine — blueberry, dogberry, or dandelion. The "home-brew," i.e., beer, and the "drop" of rum was only served to the male visitors, though both the wine and the beer were very likely brewed by the women.

Dogberry trees [*pyrus americana*] were found in many house yards, and they also grew wild near the settlement. Anyone could have dogberry wine, and most people did. Winemakers liked to gather the berries after the first frost, so as to have the most flavourful wine. Dandelion wine was not so common. This was probably because it had to be made in summer when the dandelions were in full bloom. Women were far too busy with other tasks at that time of the year to go wine making.

On New Year's Day the meals, especially the dinner, were almost as good as those served on Christmas Day. But supper on New Year's Day was often taken out of the house, at the "Orangeman's Time," which is described more fully in the next chapter.

There were other seasons of the year when special foods were eaten, but often eating practices differed according to religious affiliation. For instance, in Elliston on Shrove Tuesday (also called Soft Tuesday), everyone ate pancakes for supper. In some of these, if there were young folk in the family, the mother would hide a ring, money, and a button. Some also added a thread and a nail. The finder of the ring would be the one to marry first, the money indicated future riches, and the button meant bachelorhood or spinsterhood. The thread and the nail indicated future work, tailoring or carpentering.

When I was a small child I once asked why we always had pancakes for supper on Shrove Tuesday and was told: "to use up the grease before the beginning of Lent." United Church and Salvation Army people gave the same reason for having pancakes, but it did not have the same significance for them, for they did not refrain from eating grease on Ash Wednesday, the first day of Lent, or on Good Friday as we Anglicans did. Instead, many of them made a special point of having "hash" (boiled potatoes and other vegetables fried in salt pork) for one meal on Ash Wednesday.

Another Elliston collector[4] suggested that the custom arose from the dropping and adding of H's common in the community. People would refer to Ash Wednesday as "Hash" Wednesday. I am told by Dr. John Widdowson, a linguist, that this is also common in folk etymology in English dialects. Thus Ash Wednesday becomes "Hash" Wednesday in local speech and with the result that in both England and Elliston people believe they should have hash on Ash Wednesday.

Lenten dinners in Anglican homes always featured fish on Wednesdays and Fridays, and all meals on Ash Wednesday and Good Friday (the first and last days of Lent) were the most meagre of the whole year. Strict Anglicans fasted till noon on those days, and dinner at noon consisted simply of salt herring or salt turbot, boiled, and potatoes — no

130

sauce, no other vegetable, no dessert. Supper was also simple, no "luxu-ries." A United Church woman, Orpah Crewe, told me they always had "jam doughboys" for supper on Good Friday. They never bothered about having fish.

On Easter Day, after the restrictions of Lent, food seemed especially rich and delicious. Breakfast on Easter morning was, without exception, the most satisfying breakfast of the year. Hard-boiled eggs were a must. Often they were the first "fresh" eggs for the year. Candy and chocolate eggs were unknown in Elliston until fairly recently. Dinner and supper on Easter Day were very similar to those served on Christmas Day.

One item present in many homes was the "vinegar plant," and vine-gar was widely used in cooking. William Crewe said:

> . . . that's what we always had while we reared our family, till on the last of it. The vinegar was stronger than what you gets now, just as strong anyway.

My informants were not sure how the vinegar plant started, but Mr. Crewe said:

> Usually you'd get a drop of vinegar from somebody and if you'd keep it long enough then a plant'd start and grow in it after a while . . .

His wife, Orpah, said that she wasn't sure, but she believed that:

> In olden days they'd get a little piece of bread, you know, about that big [two inches square] and a part of a cake of yeast, not the yeast we uses now, but the dry yeast, the square, and put that in the bottle and leave it alone and after a time the plant'd grow there.

> And it'd grow that big! Sometimes you'd have to take it out and clean 'n. Take the skin off 'm, you know like a rind.

They compared the shape of the vinegar plant to a "Squid-squaw," a jelly fish. But:

> It was not white like the "squid-squaw." 'Twas tough. I used to take out the one we had in the bottle and take the little bit of top skin

off it. Peel it over. It couldn't grow so well. You'd peel 'n over a little you know. Take 'n out on a plate and take the peel off with a knife and then it'd grow.

The vinegar used to be lovely. Better than we buy now. You'd use all your vinegar till you'd have a couple of spoonfuls, no more than that, down in the bottom of your crock, whatever you'd have it in. And put sugar and water in that. A week from the time you put it in, you were able to drink that.


HEALTH CARE

In addition to their other household duties, women took care of the health needs of their families. This was probably because many of the old-time cures used common household items, or things that the housewife grew in her garden, or which grew wild in or near the community.

People in the old days were great believers in tonics. Those obtained by steeping "wild cherry bark" [*prunus pennsylvanica*], or from "ground juniper" [*juniperus communis*], were taken to insure general well-being. The roots of the "dock" [*heracleum maximum*] (burdock, a nuisance plant in most meadows) were steeped out and taken as a cure for boils. "Chucky plums" [*prunus virginiana*] and "sasprilla berries" [*aralia hispida*] were both mentioned as cures for eczema. Most gardens held mints, both peppermint and spearmint. Women stored these for winter use. They steeped the dried leaves as they would tea. This "mint tea" was used as a tonic, to cure indigestion, and for colic in babies. And black currant jam was always kept for use when someone had a sore throat. A "shallot" or a garlic placed in the ear was a common cure for earache. As Edwin Baker said: "They believed in the Bible saying: 'In the leaves of the trees shall be the healing of the nations.' "[5]

Common food items and other necessities found in every home figured in a lot of cures and preventives. Bread was used in several cures. For boils, bread poultices made by soaking stale bread in boiling water, were applied to the affected area, and held in place by gauze or a clean rag. Splinters that had caused an infection were "drawn out" with bread poultices. When they used linseed meal poultices to treat pneumonia, the hot linseed meal was placed between two layers of bread, so that the flesh would not be burned.

Molasses was another household staple which figured in a variety of

132

cures. A mixture of molasses and soap was often put on boils to "draw the core." Molasses in its pure state was used by some people to cure cuts, and several informants spoke of having big cuts healed with molasses. Such cures were also known by the men, as the following incident related by William Crewe indicates:

> We was plankin' a boat up there see, and I was spilin' the plank with the drawin' knife and had me hand like that, spilin' and he [his brother] took holt and give it the pluck, and the knife went along and took me finger and sawed 'um down there . . . There's the mark there now where I cut it . . . And it didn't seem to be gettin' well and this old man, Dicky Tucker, he came in and he done 'n up in molasses and he told me not to open 'n for I believe it was a week without opening 'n. When I opened 'n he was pretty well well. Nothing but the pure molasses, plenty of it.

Sore throats were also treated with molasses, and it was used in the candy that many women gave their children who had colds. They mixed molasses, kerosene and pepper together and boiled the mixture on the stove. This was removed from the heat and allowed to harden a bit, after which it was formed into balls and then rolled in butter. Nina Pearce told me that for those children who ordinarily got little candy, it was a treat to have a cold.

Most mothers in the early 1900s also believed that children should take "something to clean the blood." So each spring they administered "sulphur and molasses" over a period of nine days. Some of my informants had to take the mixture nine days running, but others took it for three, stopped for three, and then took it for three more days.

Snow blindness was treated with tea leaf poultices. Orpah Crewe said:

> I've seen my brother do that. Take a potful of tea and strain off . . . he'd take the leaves out of the teapot, all he could get and make a poultice with a cloth and put on his eyes and lie down for so long. And then take that off and put on another one. The only thing he could find to cure his eyes when he'd get snow blind. Take the burn out.

For night blindness, a common ailment, people were given cod liver, either raw or roasted. This cure was often administered by the men; it was known by children too. I remember once a bunch of us made a fire on Long Point in Maberly, to roast cod livers. One of the boys suffered from night blindness, and we decided to cure him. Everyone had a taste of the roasted liver. It was terrible! It made me quite sick.

Ordinary baking soda was used for treating hives, insect bites, stings, and burns. Oatmeal water was used to take the heat out of sunburn, and brown paper or a cloth dipped in vinegar was the common treatment for a headache; the saturated paper or cloth being placed on the forehead. Someone troubled with "gas" drank hot water, or hot water with a little peppermint added. Cold water was thrown over a person who had fainted, and a frost bite was rubbed with snow.

Olive oil was used in the treatment of burns, and for earache some women put warm olive oil on "tow" (cotton wool), and placed it in the ear. Some women, to cure an earache, simply blew in the child's ear, but others enlisted help from the men. Several informants, among them William Crewe, said that blowing smoke into a child's ear nine times was a cure for the earache. Hiccups stopped if you drank nine mouthfuls of cold water. Sties on the eye were rubbed with a gold ring, usually a wedding ring, for nine successive mornings, or else the child had to look through the keyhole in the door, nine times, for nine mornings.

Yarn, another item found in all households, was widely used in folk cures. Blisters were pricked open with a darning needle and then "spun yarn" was pulled through to soak up the water gathered inside. Since women used no hand lotions in the early days, and their hands were often exposed in cold weather, especially when hanging out the family wash, they were often bothered with chaps in their fingers. They eased the pain caused by these by putting "spun yarn" treated with a little vaseline in the chap, i.e., in the cracked area. Yarn was also used for treating sprained wrists, being wound tightly round the wrist. To prevent "water pups" when they were fishing, men would have yarn wound around nine times where the oil clothes chafed their wrists.

Household items also figured in "charms" (amulets), which were worn as cures. Green ribbon was mentioned by several of my informants as being a "present cure" for nosebleeds. This had to be given by someone other than a family member, and the donor could not be thanked. The nosebleed sufferer wore the ribbon around his neck, or pinned to some article of clothing near the neck. Mr. and Mrs. William Crewe were discussing someone they knew who used to suffer a lot from nosebleed:

That fellow had a good lot out of his nose. All the time subject to bleedin'.

Yes, yes. I had to give him a piece of green ribbon. That's a cure for nosebleed. I went to the store and gave it to Nina to give to him. And he never bleed the nose for years. And one time he went away in the lumberwoods and he forgot the piece of ribbon and his nose would start to bleed after he went away. Said he'd never forget his green ribbon no more.

Potatoes were worn around the neck or carried in a pocket as a cure for arthritis, or rheumatism (a term covering various pains). A nutmeg, wrapped in some cloth and worn round the neck, was a cure for boils, provided it was given by an outsider and the sufferer did not know what the charm consisted of.

Both men and women could "put away" warts, and according to my informants there was a variety of different methods practiced. They ranged from putting the same number of stones as you had warts in a package and leaving the package where someone else would find it, to tying the same number of knots as you had warts, in a string and putting the string where it would rot away. Every method suggested was known to have worked. One must have worked for me for when I was about twelve years old my hands were full of ugly warts. I used to hide my hands from sight as much as possible. One day a man in Maberly told me he'd put my warts away. A short while after, my hands were indeed wart free.

Men set any broken bones. Men also attended to any major cuts; but looking after small bruises and cuts was mainly the woman's responsibility. People used "murre" or the turpentine "bladders" found on the bark of fir trees ("starrigans") to dress a major cut. (I guess the turpentine running from these bladders gave rise to the common name for a fir tree — "snotty var"). Once my brother Clifford fell over a cliff by the swimming hole. He received several bad cuts to his head, but no broken bones. Two local men, Aubrey Pearce and Ernest Chaulk, treated his cuts with murre. They did a good job. His cuts healed leaving only faint scars.

This chapter shows clearly, I believe, that a woman's usual household tasks were enough to fill a normal day for most of the year. Nevertheless she was expected to take part in numerous ways in the community activities described in the following chapter.

# Chapter 7
## The Woman in the Community

### IN SICKNESS AND IN HEALTH

Although for the majority of women nursing activity did not extend beyond their own households, still they sometimes became involved outside the home. Anyone who had been sick for a long time would be sent hot soup, special tidbits, a share of a special meal — anything the neighbouring cooks felt would tempt the invalid's appetite. In addition, if a person were bedridden and the family could not cope with the situation themselves, the neighbourhood women "pitched in and helped."

When death came to any household the women of the community were especially involved, as they were at times of childbirth and at weddings.

A funeral in the community, like a wedding, was an important social occasion involving everyone, and the woman's role on this occasion, as in happier circumstances, was an extension of her family tasks of housekeeping and supplying personal care, food, and clothing. As in all community events, men and women did their respective jobs according to tradition.

As soon as possible after a death occurred, the deceased was "laid out." This duty was usually performed by next-door nieghbours, though certain people were called upon regularly to help. Women laid out a woman, and men looked after a man. In preparing the corpse they would tie a white cloth or napkin around the jaws and head to keep the mouth closed, and close the eyes, sometimes laying large Newfoundland pennies on them.

136

In the old days, after the body was washed, it was attired in special grave clothes. Most people were quite concerned with cutting a good figure at the last, even though they were "lay figures" in this final social activity. Some people had their grave clothes ready for years before their deaths. For women these consisted of chemise, bloomers, stockings, and white nightgown; men were buried in their best clothes, usually their Sunday suit. My great-aunt Annie, who died at the age of eighty-four in 1941, had her outfit ready for so long that the white nightdress had been washed twenty or thirty times to keep it from yellowing. The idea of having one's grave clothes ready was still held by some younger married women in the '30s. Aunt Hilda told me of a young teenage girl who was given some article of clothing as a gift. Sometime later, when her mother was asked if it fitted all right, the mother replied: "Oh yes, but it was too good for her to wear. I put it away for her grave clothes."

Once the body had been prepared for burial, it was laid out in the best room in the house, the parlour. Generally, the body was laid on a table in the centre of the room, feet pointing toward the East. If the table were not long enough, three or four boards would be placed under the body on the table. Sometimes a door would be pressed into service, and sometimes a wooden settle. White sheets were placed over the body and under it. These sheets, made of linen or shirting, were kept by most housewives in the old days specifically for laying out members of the family.

The laying out would take less than an hour to complete. Members of the immediate family would stay in another room until it was finished; then they might come to view the corpse. For the "staying-up" period, the house, especially the kitchen and parlour, was given a thorough cleaning by the women living nearby. One old lady in Elliston, about thirty to forty years ago, did not let her neighbours perform this task for her. Her husband died one day in the fall, when all the neighbours were busy digging their potatoes. I was told, "She not only laid him out, but she also gave her house a good cleaning." When she had finished all this, she walked to the nearest of the gardens and informed those working there that her husband had "passed away" that morning.

Neighbours came voluntarily to stay up, and ordinary household tasks were looked after by friends and relatives. Meals for the family were prepared by the women and brought to the house, domestic animals were cared for, and wood and water were brought into the house.

It was generally the more mature people of the settlement who stayed up with the corpse at night. Very old or sickly people would come to offer sympathy, but they would not make a protracted stay, and they usually visited by day. Children were not involved, unless the death was in the family, although they might be sent along to the house of mourning during the day with a flower for the coffin. All who visited would be asked if they wished to view the corpse. It was a widespread belief that if you viewed the corpse, you would not think about it later.

Both men and women stayed up in the house of mourning and although it was a very solemn occasion, the atmosphere varied according to the age of the deceased, length of illness, and the personalities of those present — the latter perhaps being the deciding factor. Quiet conversation was the only accepted way of passing the time, but occasionally the group was noisier. There was no singing, but they might tell jokes, or reminisce about the deceased and tell anecdotes about things he had said or done.

Although there was no entertainment, there were some amusing incidents. For instance, on one occasion, two of my Mother's aunts were staying up in a home where an old lady had passed away. Her husband was a bit odd, and part way through the night he went into the room where the corpse was lying and removed the pillow from under her head. He came back to the kitchen, placed the pillow on the hard wooden settle, and proceeded to go to sleep. Those present were shocked beyond measure, and perhaps a bit frightened. He reassured them by saying: "Martha, pore ol' soul, can't hurt me now, she's dead. Anyway, she'd rather for me to have it." Off he went to sleep, but there was no sleep for the others in the room. This was just as well, anyway, since someone was expected to stay awake all through the night.

The women served a cup of tea and something light to eat to those who stayed up. This was served in the kitchen where all the people were gathered. No one stayed in the room with the corpse, but a light was left burning there.

During the period between death and burial, the acknowledged carpenters in the community were asked to make the coffin and did so without charging for their services, using wood purchased from the local merchant by the family of the deceased. One man, Edwin Baker, must have made hundreds during his lifetime. He had his own coffin ready years before he died.

In earlier days, coffins were made plain with flat covers, but more recently were made with raised covers. Poorer families might not have as costly materials as those better off: for instance, rope handles might have to serve instead of ornate metal handles. The outside of each coffin was covered with a brocade-style material. There was a wide variation in the colour chosen for this covering. Old people would have dark purple; the middle aged, deep blue; young adults, pale blue; children, white. For members of the Orange Society, the coffin would be covered in a colour which distinguished their "degree" in that society.

All coffins were lined inside with shirting or sateen. Around the rim, where the cover was thrown back, it was trimmed with "full mountain," a gold or black material, heavier than present day tinfoil. It was fastened to the rim with tacks. Children's coffins were often trimmed with lace instead of full mountain. My great-grandmother Tilly did not want full mountain round her box, for she said it made a coffin look too much like a trunk. When she died her coffin was trimmed with lace.

For the funeral, if a person were especially well-liked, the coffin would be covered with flowers, always artificial ones with perhaps the addition of some real ones in summer. Certain women in the community were skilled in making crepe-paper flowers. They were kept busy during the period between death and burial preparing "sprays" for the coffin. Women who had flower gardens made floral wreaths. They arranged and then sewed the fresh flowers on heavy cardboard circular frames. I remember Mother making such wreaths. My brother Cliff and I used to make our own wreaths from the scraps she had left over. These we would place on Uncle Walt's dog, Pomp, as he lay on the floor "dead." Women fastened the floral tributes to the coffin. They used tacks in the old days, but in more recent times, tape.

The funeral normally took place on the third day after the death, unless for medical reasons the period was shortened. During these three days the women who were looking after matters in the house of mourning would have made up white linen bands, which would be delivered to the head of each household. At the funeral the men wore them pinned on the left sleeve above the elbow. The pallbearers also wore white scarves, but they were longer, with the ends flowing free.

In Elliston, it was customary for both men and women to attend funerals, though it was rare for a woman to attend the burial of her husband or child. Women do not ordinarily carry the coffin. My informants, however, remembered one occasion when little girls acted as pallbearers. A tiny girl of two, buried by the Salvation Army, was carried by four little girls dressed in white. Men are normally chosen for the task of bearing the corpse. In the old days this was no light job.

In summer coffins were carried by means of the handles affixed to the

139

sides of the coffin. Those who had to move a corpse a long distance (say from the North Side or from Maberly / one and a half to two miles from the church) received help from the men in the funeral procession. They would step forward in twos and take their turns bearing the corpse. This changeover was effected without any stoppage in the onward movement of the procession. In winter the coffin would be drawn to the church on a "slide."

All who went to the funeral were sombrely dressed and the number attending was usually a good indication of the popularity of the deceased. For some the church would be crowded; for others there would only be the immediate relatives. During the church service the chief mourners sat all the way through.

It was the custom for the bereaved family to attend church as official mourners for three consecutive Sundays after the funeral, sitting through-out the service on each occasion.[1]

Each adult member of the bereaved family wore a black band on the left sleeve for months after the death. Widows wore black every day for months and even years after their husbands died.


CHURCH WORK

All through the year the women of Elliston were active in church work. The Methodist (United Church) Ladies Aid, begun in the 1920s, or-ganized events to raise money for the Church; looked after the "Parson-age," i.e., the minister's residence; welcomed new ministers and their fam-ilies to the community; and saw that everything at the parsonage was in readiness for the new occupants. Anglican women in Elliston did not form an organization but interested Church members, usually from the churchwarden's household, were responsible for the "church housekeep-ing," that is, the changing of the altar cloths with the changing church sea-sons, and weekly dusting.

The church got a thorough cleaning once a year. A certain afternoon, usually in late spring, was appointed for cleaning day, and all the women of the congregation were expected to turn up at the church with their cleaning equipment — scrubbing brushes, buckets, soap, water, and cleaning rags. Anyone unable or unwilling to do her share of the scrub-bing was expected to pay another woman to clean for her.

Anglican women in Elliston were involved with church work at the housekeeping level, and in one case, as I learned from N.C. Crewe's "File on Elliston," a woman actually assisted in the church services:

Elizabeth (Mrs. Mark Way), the eldest sister of Arthur Tilly (daughter of Robert Tilly) first married to James Baker, outliving both her husbands, lost both her children in childhood, a woman of natural refinement, was licensed to conduct services in the Anglican Church at Elliston, the only female lay reader I ever heard of.[2]

## SOCIAL EVENTS

In addition to their various services to their neighbours and the church, women were also the prime movers in the major social occasions of the year. In Elliston, as in most small outports, the church was the centre of community life, and almost all the social events were church or church-school sponsored. The major occasions were the Sunday School picnics, the "times," the concerts, and (from the 1930s onwards) the garden parties.

Picnics in the early 1900s all started in the afternoon, and in Maberly they were preceded by a parade of Sunday School pupils around the community: the boys carrying flags, the girls with "wreaths" (flowers fastened to a circular or square wooden frame attached to a long handle). At the picnic the children took part in competitive sports, chiefly racing and jumping. The winners received small prizes. Ring games were also played at picnics. Candy was thrown up in the air by the handful and every child scrambled for his share.

Parents and other adults would come later in the afternoon to serve and eat some picnic food. The women had to be very sure they had baked lots of cakes and pies so that everyone might be given a "cup of tea." Anyone who cared to could attend. There was never any charge for the food served at a picnic. One woman, Emily (Pearce) Tilley, mentioned baking "trunks of cakes" for one such occasion.

Picnics were still being held in the Thirties and Forties, but they were not exactly the same as those held in the early 1900s. They became strictly children's affairs. The only adults that took part were the minister and the Sunday School teacher or teachers. Serving lunch was not the big event it had been: children just carried enough for themselves.

The old-time picnic, involving the whole community, was replaced in the late 1930s by the Garden Party. The Anglican and United Church congregations held garden parties annually until the 1960s. At these, patrons paid for their meals and for the entertainments. There were different games and competitions: games of chance and skill, such as bowling, pitching pennies, and fish pond; and games of guessing. Prizes were designed to tempt a person to participate. All prizes were donated by local business firms, or by interested persons.

Sometimes these affairs were kept up for two nights. On the first night a substantial "cold plate" would be served. Meat would be served on individual plates; but salads of all sorts: potato, tossed greens, jelly, and others, would be in serving dishes on the table. Whole cakes, pies, and tarts would be laid on the table in front of the diners, so that they could help themselves. Assorted dishes of cookies would be placed at convenient intervals.

Most of the interested women of the congretation would be involved in catering; and there would be keen, though unspoken, rivalry as to who set the best table, as each woman was responsible for a certain section of the long table. People in the know always wanted to sit at Mrs. So-and-So's table because her food was always delicious; they would avoid another woman's table because her food was not so mouth watering. Sometimes to get around this rivalry, those in charge of the affair had contributions from different women all mixed together, and the woman responsible for serving tea on a certain table might have none of her own cakes on it. On the second night, instead of a cold plate, the women usually served a substantial vegetable soup, along with tea and cake and cookies as on the previous night.

The success of any garden party or social gathering where food was to be served depended on the women, for men had nothing to do with cooking or serving.

The men, however, had much to contribute. It was they who erected the rough dining tables, collected the admission tickets at the door or gate, boiled the water for the dishwashing, and managed the outside entertainments — the bowling, fish pond, darts, etc. Without the co-operation of both sexes, a garden party could not have been held.

The same collaboration was necessary for the annual Orangemen's "time" held on New Year's Day. In Elliston the majority of the men were Lodge members, and their wives, sisters, or mothers, supplied and served the supper, working under extremely difficult conditions. The area reserved for the kitchen in the Orange Hall used to be a room about ten feet square, furnished with one iron cook stove. Its top would be packed with tea kettles. If soup was being served, pots of soup would have to be placed on or about the stove as well. Dishes were washed in pans at the counter in the same room, but there was no running water, hot or cold. Hot water for dish washing was heated in a big tank over an open fire that was kindled on the grounds just outside the building. How they managed to serve hot tea or anything else hot is hard to imagine; but they did, admirably.

Women were, of course, deeply involved in all the other events of the Christmas season. Their domestic role in providing festive foods, home-made wines, and in readying their houses for visitors has already been described (Chapter Six). But some of the women also took an active part in "getting up" and "putting off" holiday concerts, consisting of dialogues, skits, individual and group songs, instrumental music, and recitations. These performances were in aid of the school or the church, and similar concerts were also presented at Easter.

And then there was mummering. Christmas would not have been Christmas before 1950 without mummers.[3] Men, women and children put on disguises and visited their neighbours, often acting in rowdy fashion, until their identities had been guessed. It was the mother's responsibility to help provide a suitable costume for each member of the family that decided to go mummering, and this probably every night of the holiday period, except Sundays and Christmas Night. Costumes were changed each night, unless the mummers planned to visit a different section of the community than that covered the previous night. Trunks and storage boxes were searched for old garments. Bed quilts particularly were in great demand.

Middle-aged or elderly married women did not often go mummering, but younger marrieds and unattached girls went out. It was true for women, as for all mummers, that once disguised they tended to take on whole new personalities. They would dance, "carry on," talk incessantly and loudly. In fact, they acted quite the opposite of their usual well-behaved, modest selves. Mummering provided a welcome outlet for many women to let loose for once, and was perhaps the only chance some got during the whole year to go visiting at night. Mainly, however, the woman's role was to be a good hostess to all mummers who came to her door, and she could not be too fussy about the amount of snow and water they tramped into her kitchen.

VISITING

There used to be a lot of informal visiting all through the year, for both men and women. After "the fall closed in" the nightly visit to a neighbour was almost a ritual with some men. In the days before radio they might listen to a book being read or tell their own stories. During the Forties they went to hear the "war news." In late spring, summer, and early fall, all the men of the community gathered in groups on Sunday mornings. They met "on the Gaze," "in the Square," and near the old Methodist graveyard, to name a few places. Here they joked, chatted, yarned, and argued. Young boys used to sit or stand beside the men and listen to what was said.

Girls and women never went near these men's groups when they were gathered for a chat. Married women did their visiting in the afternoon, when the children were in school and the men away working. Young unmarried women, however, visited around the neighbourhood at night in the wintertime. They always brought their knitting, crocheting, or embroidery with them, and worked as they joked, chatted, and told or listened to stories. Even when they were socializing, women's fingers were never idle.

*   *   *   *   *

A woman in Elliston led a full and satisfying life. She worked hard, but she was not a slave. She was her husband's partner, more than fifty percent — the mainstay of the family.

# Notes

*Introduction*

1. I found the questionnaires I obtained from the Memorial University of Newfoundland Folklore and Language Archive on "Folk Medicine," "The Folktale," and "The Old Hag," extremely useful as guides for questioning on these topics. For information on death and funeral customs I used the pertinent chapter in *A Handbook of Irish Folklore* by Seán Ó Súilleabháin (1942; rpt. Hatboro, Pa.: Folklore Associates, 1963); this is the comprehensive manual used by the collectors of the Irish Folklore Commission and gives questions designed to elicit information across the whole spectrum of folklore and folklife.

For beliefs and superstitions I used a finding list based on volume six of Wayland D. Hand's *Popular Beliefs and Superstitions of North Carolina*, in *The Frank C. Brown Collection of North Carolina Folklore* (Durham, N.C.: Duke University Press, 1961). This is part of the standard work on this subject for the English-language tradition. Since Hand has numbered each item successively, my references are to Hand, No. . . . . Where Hand items are cited, his notes indicate that this phrasing of the belief is found in other English-speaking areas of North America.

*Chapter 1. The Community: Elliston*

1. The name was changed from Bird Island Cove to Elliston in the early 1900s through the efforts of a Methodist clergyman, Reverend

145

Charles Lench. It was done to commemorate the first visit of a Methodist missionary to the community in 1814, an Irishman named Ellis.

2. Checking through Dr. Keith Matthews' *A "Who Was Who" of Families Engaged in the Fishery and Settlement of Newfoundland 1660–1840* (Memorial University of Newfoundland, 1971), I found that many Elliston names were overwhelmingly West Country in origin — Dorset, Devon, Somerset, and to a lesser extent, Cornwall.

3. Order given by Governor Shuldham, St. John's, October 7, 1774, p. 220, Vol. S1, 5. Copied from Mr. N. C. Crewe's "Elliston File", Provincial Archives, St. John's, Newfoundland.

4. Information copied from Church of England Bonavista Church Records, Births, Marriages, and Deaths, 1786–1834.

5. Information copied from Mr. N. C. Crewe's "Elliston File," Provincial Archives, St. John's.

6. *House of Assembly Journal*, 1859, Education Report, Appendix, p. 255.

7. Excerpt from a letter written by William Kelson, November 18, 1814. Slade Letter Book, "Slade File," Provincial Archives, St. John's.

8. Charles Lench, *The Story of Methodism in Bonavista* (St. John's, 1919), p. 142.

9. Philip Tocque, *Wandering Thoughts* (London, 1846), p. 118.

10. Ernest Tilly, "Memories of an Oldtimer," *The Newfoundland Quarterly*, 57, No. 1 (1958), 39.

11. Charles Lench, *The Story of Methodism in Bonavista*, p. 17.

*Chapter 2.    Making a Living: "The Woman Was More Than 50%"*
1. If the trip contained more than one boatload of fish, the remainder was "bagged", that is, channelled into a "net bag" which was then attached to the stern of the small boat or "rodney." This was left at the trapsite. Second or third boatloads or more could be "dipped out" (using dip nets) very easily.

2. Alice Morse Earle, *Home Life in Colonial Days* (New York, 1898), pp. 194–196, has an excellent description of "carding" as done in old New England.

*Chapter 3.    Girlhood: The Learning Years*
1. John C. Campbell, *The Southern Highlander and His Homeland* (New York, 1921), p. 124.

2. I saw two Newfoundland examples of these knife boards during

the summer of 1970. One was in the Trinity Museum at Trinity, T.B., and the other in the little "Folk Museum" in Bonavista, B.B.

3. Flora Thompson, *Lark Rise to Candleford* (London, 1946), p. 158.

4. Alice Morse Earle, *Home Life in Colonial Days*, p. 261: " . . . girls were taught to knit, as soon as their little hands could hold the needles. Sometimes girls four years of age could knit stockings."

5. The same style is mentioned by Sybil Marshall, *Fenland Chronicle* (Cambridge, 1967), p. 163. She says: "hair . . . had been washed the night before and braided into dozens of tiny plaits, so that the next morning it would be all frizzed and crimped."

6. Alice Morse Earle, *Home Life in Colonial Days*, p. 323.

7. Sybil Marshall, *Fenland Chronicle*, p. 196, says that in Cambridgeshire: (they would) "run squealing away at the sight of the long blue, green and red "darning needles' or' sew-your-eyes up', as we called the dragonflies." Alice Morse Earle, *Child Life in Colonial Days* (New York, 1899), p. 399 says: "We believed . . . that dragon-flies flew with the sole thought of sewing up our lips — devil's darning-needles we called them. To this day I instinctively cover my mouth at their approach."

8. Alice Morse Earle, *Child Life in Colonial Days*, p. 399: "We believed that earwigs lived for the sole purpose of penetrating our ears."

9. A similar rhyme is reported from West Somerset but there it is addressed not to the slug but to the snail, which in that dialect is called a "snarley-horn." See G. F. Northall, *English Folk-Rhymes* (London, 1892), p. 328. A Gaelic salute was: "Seilcheag, seilcheag, cuir a mach do chluasan/Air neo marbhaidh mi thu." (Snail, snail, put out your horn/Or I will beat you to death.)

10. A. M. Earle speaks of the flower lore of New England children in *Child Life in Colonial Days*, pp. 380–387: the making of dandelion chains; the plucking of the petals of the ox-eye daisy to the refrain of "he loves me, he loves me not"; the making of leafy boats from the broad leaves of the "flower-de-luce" with the added touch of pansies for crew; the nibbling of sorrel leaves or "sour grass."

And in the Cambridgeshire fens children also used nature's materials. See Sybil Marshall, *Fenland Chronicle*, p. 195: "Feathery reeds stood above our heads, and we used to pull the pointed leaves of 'em for two purposes. If you laid the flat leaf tight atween the two palms o' your hands, and blowed short and sharp on it in a certain way, you could make a piercing shriek of a whistle as 'ould tear your eardrums, and if you knowed how you could make a real little boat that 'ould sail up the dyke, out of one of the leaves."

11. See Alice Bertha Gomme, *The Traditional Games of England, Scotland, and Ireland* (New York, 1964), II, 149-179, for other versions of the rhyme.

12. *Ibid.*, I, 404–407

13. *Ibid.*, pp. 223–227. Cf. Fig. 3.

14. *Ibid.*, pp. 122–129. "Fivestones." Sybil Marshall in "Mam's Book," *Fenland Chronicle*, p. 187, says: "the girls played 'jinks' with five stones." And A. M. Earle in *Child Life in Colonial Days*, p. 372, says: "Jackstones was an old English game known in Locke's day as dibstones. Other names for the game were chuckstones, chuckie-stones, and clinches. The game is precisely the same as it was played two centuries ago; it was a girl's game then — it is a girl's game now." There is also an excellent description of the game in John Symonds Udal, *Dorsetshire Folk-Lore* (Hertford, 1922), p. 325.

15. Versions of this game may be found in Norman Wymer, *Village Life* (London (1951)), p. 147, and in Udal, *Dorsetshire Folk-Lore*, pp. 370–371.

16. Cf. Udal, *Dorsetshire Folk-Lore*, p. 373 "Duck-stone."

17. Cf. Gomme, *The Traditional Games of England, Scotland, and Ireland*, II, 14-15, "Old Dame."

*Chapter 4. The Young Woman: Courtship and Marriage*

1. The same prudery was observed in Oxfordshire at the turn of the century as is expressed by Flora Thompson in *Lark Rise to Candleford*, pp. 512–513, " . . . Miss Lane's more personal intimate wear dried modestly on a line by the henhouse, 'out of the men's sight.' "

2. Cf. Alice Bertha Gomme, *The Traditional Games of England, Scotland and Ireland*, I, 302–304.

3. *Ibid.*, pp. 289–293.

4. Cf. Hand, No. 4665-4666.

5. Cf. Hand, No. 4284.

6. Cf. Hand, No. 4629: "If you fall up the steps, you won't be married for a year."

7. Cf. Hand, No. 4411-4412.

8. Cf. Hand, No. 4743. This has no mention of throwing the egg on the roadway.

9. Cf. Hand, No. 4540, which mentions a snail tracing out the initials.

10. Cf. Hand, No. 4536-4539, which mentions snails tracing initials in meal or flour on May 1st.

11. A very similar practice on Midsummer Eve is mentioned by John Symonds Udal, *Dorsetshire Folk-Lore*, pp. 46–47. Also see notes to Hand, No. 4304.

12. Udal, Dorsetshire Folklore, p. 45, describes the rite and gives the following rhyme:

'Hemp-seed I set, hemp-seed I sow,

The man that is my true-love come after me and mow."

13. Cf. Hand, No. 4801, 4802, 4803.

14. Cf. Wayman Hogue, *Back Yonder* (New York, 1932), p. 98. A wedding ring, fashioned from a dime, was used in his community in the Ozarks when he was a lad.

15. Cf. Hand, No. 4771.

16. Cf. Hand, No. 4773.

17. John Symonds Udal, *Dorsetshire Folk-Lore*, p. 191.

*Chapter 5.  The Woman and Her Family: Pregnancy, Childbirth, and Infant Care*

1. Cf. Hand, No. 169.

2. Cf. Hand, No. 98, 99.

3. Cf. Hand, No. 86, 96.

4. Cf. Hand, No. 83, 84.

5. For other methods of removing birthmarks cf. Hand, No. 87.

6. Cf. Hand, No. 114.

7. A full discussion of this and related beliefs is in Herbert Halpert, "Legends of the Cursed Child," *New York Folklore Quarterly*, 14 (1958), 233–241; also reprinted in *Whatever Makes Papa Laugh*, Warren S. Walker, ed. (Cooperstown, N.Y., 1958), pp. 73-81. Cf. also Hand, Nos. 116, 117, 120.

8. Cf. Hand, No. 6.

9. I could find no exact parallel in Hand, No. 6, where he mentions the spring, the creek, and the well as places in which the family doctor found children.

10. Rev. George Patterson, "Notes on the Dialect of the People of Newfoundland," *Journal of American Folklore*, 9 (1896), 22.

11. Alice Morse Earle, *Child Life in Colonial Days*, p. 17.

12. George Allen England, "Newfoundland Dialect Items," *Dialect Notes*, 5 (1925), 333.

13. I could not find a specific parallel to this "long life" belief in Hand; but John Symonds Udal, *Dorsetshire Folk-Lore*, p. 178, has the following: "It is considered a good sign if an infant cries at his baptism. If it remains quiet and passive it is said to be 'too good to live'."

14. Alice Morse Earle, *Child Life in Colonial Days*, p. 13.

15. Cf. Hand, No. 163.

16. Cf. Hand, No. 267.

17. Cf. Hand, No. 320, which gives a different cure for "white mouth."

18. Cf. Hand, Nos. 227, 232, 233.

19. Cf. Hand, Nos. 355-380, *Passim*. Most of these refer to charms worn around the baby's neck, but there is no mention of lobster shells. No. 375 states "the gums of a teething child should be rubbed with a silver thimble."

20. Cf. Hand, No. 264.

21. This word, variously spelled "whittles", "whetals", "whittals", "widdles" was, according to sources quoted in the *English Dialect Dictionary*, found in various parts of England: Warwickshire, Gloucestershire, West Somerset, Cornwall, Dorset, and North Devon. All referred to a similar way of dressing a baby.

*Chapter 6.   The Woman and her Home*

1. Philip Tocque, *Wandering Thoughts* (London, 1846), p. 323.

2. Mrs. Maud Hobbs showed me the "box iron" which her mother used in the early 1900s. There is also a "box iron" on display in the Provincial Museum, Duckworth Street, St. John's.

3. Cf. Hand, No. 2834.

4. Memorial University of Newfoundland Folklore and Language Archive, Collection 69-17, p. 88.

5. *Revelation*, 22. 2: "In the midst of the street of it, and on either side of the river, was there the tree of life, which bare twelve manner of fruits, and yielded her fruit every month: and the leaves of the tree were for the healing of the nations."

*Chapter 7.   The Woman in the Community*

1. The same practice was followed in Dorset, see John Symonds Udal, *Dorsetshire Folk-Lore*, p. 187.

2. N.C. Crewe, "Elliston File," Provincial Archives, St. John's.

3. For a full discussion of mummers, see Herbert Halpert and G. M. Story, eds., *Christmas Mumming in Newfoundland* (Toronto, 1969).

# Bibliography

Campbell, John C. *The Southern Highlander and His Homeland*. New York: Russell Sage Foundation, 1921.

Earle, Alice Morse. *Child Life in Colonial Days*. New York: The Macmillan Company, 1899.

Earle, Alice Morse. *Home Life in Colonial Days*. New York: The Macmillan Company, 1898.

England, George Allen. "Newfoundland Dialect Items," *Dialect Notes*, 5 (1925), 322–346.

Firestone, Melvin M. "The Structure of Crews," in his *Brothers and Rivals: Patrilocality in Savage Cove*. Newfoundland Social and Economic Studies No. 5. St. John's: Institute of Social and Economic Research, Memorial University of Newfoundland, 1967, pp. 45–61.

Gomme, Alice Bertha. *The Traditional Games of England, Scotland, and Ireland*. 2 vols. London, 1894–98; rpt. New York: Dover Publications, Inc., 1964.

Halpert, Herbert and G. M. Story, eds. *Christmas Mumming in Newfoundland. Essays in Anthropology, Folklore, and History*. (Toronto): Published for Memorial University of Newfoundland by University of Toronto Press, 1969.

Halpert, Herbert. "Legends of the Cursed Child," *New York Folklore Quarterly*, 14 (1958), 233–241. Also reprinted in *Whatever Makes Papa Laugh*, ed. Warren S. Walker. Cooperstown, N.Y.: New York Folklore Society, 1958, pp. 73-81.

Hand, Wayland D., ed. *Popular Beliefs and Superstitutions of North Carolina*, in The Frank C. Brown Collection of North Carolina Folklore, ed. N.I. White and others. Durham, N.C.: Duke University Press, 1961, Vol. 6.

Hitchcock, Roswell D., ed. *The Analytical Reference Bible*. New York and London: Funk & Wagnalls Company, 1918.

Hogue, Wayman. *Back Yonder. An Ozark Chronicle*. New York: Minton, Balch & Company, 1932.

Lench, Charles. *The Story of Methodism in Bonavista*. 2nd ed. St. John's: Robinson & Company, Limited, Printers, 1919.

Marshall, Sybil. *Fenland Chronicle*. Cambridge: The University Press, 1967.

Matthews, Keith. *A "Who Was Who" of Families Engaged in the Fishery and Settlement of Newfoundland, 1960–1840*. (St. John's): Memorial University of Newfoundland, 1971.

Murray, James A. H., *et al.*, eds. *The Oxford English Dictionary*. Oxford: The Clarendon Press, 1961.

Newfoundland. General Assembly. *Journal of the House of Assembly of Newfoundland*, 1859, Education Report.

Northall, G. F. *English Folk-Rhymes*. London: Kegan Paul, Trench, Trübner & Co., Ltd., 1892.

O Suilleabhain, Sean. *A Handbook of Irish Folklore*. Dublin, 1942; rpt. Hatboro, Pa.: Folklore Associates, Inc., 1963.

Patterson, George. "Notes on the Dialect of the People of Newfoundland," *Journal of American Folklore*, 9 (1896) 19–37.

Rowe, F. W. *The History of Education in Newfoundland*. Toronto: Ryerson Press, 1952.

Thompson, Flora. *Lark Rise to Candleford*. London: Oxford University Press, 1946.

Tilly, Ernest. "Memories of an Oldtimer," *The Newfoundland Quarterly*, 57, No. 1 (1958), 14, 16, 39–41, 43.

Tocque, Philip. *Wandering Thoughts*. London: Thomas Richardson and Son, 1846.

Udal, John Symonds. *Dorsetshire Folk-Lore*. Hertford, 1922; rpt. St. Peter Port, Guernsey: Toucan Press, 1970.

Wright, Joseph, ed. *The English Dialect Dictionary*. 6 vols. London: Henry Frowde, 1898–1905.

Wymer, Norman. *Village Life*. London: George G. Harrap & Co. Ltd., 1951.

## ARCHIVAL SOURCES

Bonavista Church Records. Church of England, Bonavista, Newfoundland. Births, Marriages, and Deaths, 1786–1834.

Memorial University of Newfoundland Folklore and Language Archive. St. John's, Newfoundland.

Newfoundland Dictionary Centre. Word Files. Memorial University of Newfoundland. St. John's, Newfoundland.

Provincial Archives. St. John's, Newfoundland. Crewe, N. C. Elliston File.

Slade Letter Book. Slade File.

# Further Reading

Works by and about women and women's part in pioneer and rural life

Abrahamson, Una. *God Bless our Home. Domestic Life in Nineteenth Century Canada* [n.p., Canada]: Burns & MacEachern Limited, 1966.

Armstrong, Audrey I. *Harness in the Parlour.* Toronto: Musson Book Company, 1974.

Banfill, B. J. *Labrador Nurse.* Philadelphia: Macrae Smith Company, 1953.

Barbour, Florence Grant. *Memories of Life on the Labrador and in Newfoundland.* A Hearthstone Book. New York: Carlton Press, Inc., 1973.

Bayne-Powell, Rosamond. *Housekeeping in the Eighteenth Century.* London: John Murray, 1956.

Blacking, John. *Black Background: The Childhood of a South African Girl.* New York: Abelard-Schuman, 1964.

Blomefield, Mathena [*pseudonym* for Mathena Victoria Day]. *The Bulley-mung Pit. The Story of a Norfolk Farmer's Child.* London: Faber and Faber Limited, 1946.

Blomefield, Mathena [*pseudonym* for Mathena Victoria Day]. *Nuts in the Rookery.* London: Faber and Faber Limited, 1946.

Bond, L.M.G. *Tyneham. A Lost Heritage.* 1956; prt. Dorchester: Longmans (Dorchester) Ltd., 1968.

Bosanquet, Rosalie E., ed. *In the Troublesome Times. The Cambo Women's Institute Book of 1922.* Newcastle upon Tyne: Northumberland Press Limited, 1929.

Bourne, George [*pseudonym* for George Sturt]. *A Farmer's Life. With a Memoir of the Farmer's Sister.* London: Jonathan Cape, 1922.

Bourne, George [*pseudonym* for George Sturt]. *Lucy Bettesworth.* London: Duckworth & Co., 1913.

Bradford, Gamaliel. *Elizabethan Women.* Ed. Harold Ogden White. 1936; rpt. Freeport, N.Y.: Books for Libraries Press, 1969.

Briggs, Jean L. *Never in Anger. Portrait of an Eskimo Family.* Cambridge, Mass.: Harvard University Press, 1970.

Call, Cora Pinkley. *Within My Ozark Valley.* Eureka Springs, Ark.: Times-Echo, 1956.

Call, Hughie. *Golden Fleece.* 1942: rpt. New York: Crown Publishers, Inc., 1961.

Campbell, Marie. *Cloud-Walking.* 1942: rpt. Bloomington and London: Indiana University Press, 1971.

Campbell, Marie. *Folks Do Get Born.* New York & Toronto: Rinehart & Company, Incorporated, 1946.

Carberry, Mary. *The Farm by Lough Gur.* The Longman Library. London: Longmans, Green and Co., 1940.

Chamberlain, Mary. *Fenwomen.* London: Virago with Quartet Books, 1975.

Chao, B. Y. *Autobiography of a Chinese Woman.* New York: The John Day Company, [1947].

Clark, Alice. *Working Life of Women in the Seventeenth Century.* London: George Routledge & Sons, Ltd., New York: E.P. Dutton & Co., 1919.

Cleaveland, Agnes Morley. *No Life for a Lady.* Boston: Houghton Mifflin Company, 1941.

Dacombe, Marianne R., ed. *Dorset: Up Along and Down Along. A Collection . . . Gathered Together by Members of Women's Institutes.* 2nd ed. Gillingham Dorset: Printed by T.H. Brickell & Son, The Blackmore Press, n.d. [1936].

Dale, Edward Everett. *Frontier Ways.* Austin: University of Texas Press, 1959.

Diack, Lesley. *Labrador Nurse.* London: Victor Gollancz Ltd., 1963.

Emery, Sarah Anna. *Reminiscences of a Nonagenarian.* Newburyport: William H. Huse & Co., Printers, 1879.

Festing, Sally. *Fishermen.* Newton Abbot: David & Charles, 1977.

Fraser, Amy Stewart. *The Hills of Home.* London and Boston: Routledge & Kegan Paul, 1973.

Fraser, Amy Stewart. *In Memory Long*. London: Routledge & Kegan Paul, 1977.

Fussell, G.E. & K.R. *The English Countrywoman. A Farmhouse Social History, A.D. 1500–1900*. London: Andrew Melrose, 1953.

Gale, Fay, ed. *Woman's Role in Aboriginal Society*. Australian Aboriginal Studies No. 36; Social Anthropology Series No. 6. Canberra: Australian Institute of Aboriginal Studies, 1970.

Gandy, Ida. *A Wiltshire Childhood*. London: George Allen & Unwin Ltd., 1929.

Goodale, Jane C. *Tiwi Wives: A Study of the Women of Melville Island, North Australia*. American Ethnological Society, Monograph 51. Seattle: University of Washington Press. 1971.:

Goudie, Elizabeth. *Woman of Labrador*. Ed. David Zimmerly. [Toronto]: Peter Martin Associates Limited, 1973.

Grant, Elizabeth, of Rothiemurchus. *Memoirs of a Highland Lady*. Ed. Lady Strachey. 1898; rpt. London: John Murray, 1928.

Grant, I.F. *Highland Folk Ways*. London: Routledge & Kegan Paul, 1961.

Green, H. Gordon. *Don't have your baby in the dory. A Biography of Myra Bennett*. [Montreal]: Harvest House, 1974.

Grenfell, Anne and Katie Spalding. *Le Petit Nord: Annals of a Labrador Harbour*. London: Hodder and Stoughton, Limited, n.d. [1920].

Guillet, Edwin C. *Pioneer Arts and Crafts*. 1940; rpt. [Toronto]: University of Toronto Press, 1968.

Hammond, Dorothy and Alta Jablow. *Women: Their Economic Role in Traditional Societies*. An Additon-Wesley Module in Anthropology, No. 35. [Reading, Mass.: Addison-Wesley Publishing Company, Inc., 1973].

Hayden, Eleanor G. *Travels Round our Village. A Berkshire Book*. Westminster: Archibald Constable & Co. Ltd., 1901.

Heath, Francis George. *Peasant Life in the West of England*. 4th ed. London: Sampson Low, Marston, Searle, & Rivington, 1881.

Hocking, Salome. *Some Old Cornish Folk*. London: Charles H. Kelly, 1903.

Hole, Christina. *English Home-Life, 1500 to 1800*. London: B.T. Batsford Ltd., 1947.

Holliday, Carl. *Woman's Life in Colonial Days*. 1922; rpt. Williamstown, Mass.: Corner House Publishers, 1968.

Horn, Pamela. *The Victorian Country Child*. Kineton: The Roundwood Press, 1974.

Howard, Dorothy. *Dorothy's World*. Englewood Cliffs, N.J.: Prentice-Hall, Inc., 1977.

Jaramillo, C.M. *Romance of a Little Village Girl*. San Antonio: Naylor Co., 1955.

Jefferies, Richard. *The Toilers of the Field*. London: Longmans, Green, and Co., 1892.

Jekyll, Gertrude and Sydney R. Jones. *Old English Household Life*. London: B.T. Batsford Ltd., 1939.

Jekyll, Gertrude. *Old West Surrey*. London: Longmans, Green, and Co., 1904.

Jordan, Charles G. *The Lure of the Old Homestead*. New York: Fleming H. Revell Company, 1934.

Kaberry, Phyllis M. *Aboriginal Woman, Sacred and Profane*. London: George Routledge and Sons, Ltd., 1939.

Kettlewell, (Mrs.) F.B. *"Trinkum-Trinkums" of Fifty Years*. Taunton: Barnicott & Pearce, The Wessex Press, 1927.

Landes, Ruth. *The Objibwa Woman*. Columbia University Contributions to Anthropology, vol. 31. 1938; rpt. New York: AMS Press, 1969.

Larcom, Lucy. *A New England Girlhood*. Boston: Houghton, Mifflin and Company, 1889.

Lurie, Nancy O. *Mountain Wolf Woman, Sister of Crashing Thunder: The Autobiography of a Winnebago Woman*. Ann Arbor, Mich.: University of Michigan Press, 1961.

Macdonald, Colin. *Echoes of the Glen*. Edinburgh & London: The Moray Press, 1936.

MacPhail, Margaret. *The Girl from Loch Bras D'Or*. Windsor: Nova Scotia: Lancelot Press, 1973.

Marriott, Alice. *Maria: The Potter of San Ildefonso*. Norman: University of Oklahoma Press, 1948.

Matthews, Sallie Reynolds. *Interwoven. A Pioneer Chronicle*. 1936; rpt. Austin & London: University of Texas Press, 1974.

Matthews, William. *British Autobiographies. An Annotated Bibliography of British Autobiographies Published or Written before 1951*. Berkeley and Los Angeles: University of California Press, 1955.

Matthews, William, comp. *Canadian Diaries and Autobiographies*. Berkeley and Los Angeles: University of California Press, 1950.

Mead, Margaret. — *From the South Seas. Studies of Adolescence and Sex in Primitive Societies*. New York: William Morrow & Company, 1939. [Includes: *Coming of Age in Samoa, Growing Up In New Guinea, Sex and Temperament*].

157

Miles, Emma B. *The Spirit of the Mountains*. New York: James Pott & Company, 1905.

Murray, Eunice G. *Scottish Women in Bygone Days*. Glasgow and London: Gowans & Gray, Ltd., 1930.

Neff, Wanda Fraiken. *Victorian Working Women*. New York: AMS Press, Inc., 1966.

Norfolk Federation of Women's Institutes, 1971, comp. *Within Living Memory. A Collection of Norfolk Reminiscences*. n.p.: Norfolk Federation of Women's Institutes, 1972.

O'Neale, Lila M. *Yurok-Karok Basket Weavers*. University of California Publications in American Archeology and Ethnology, 32, No. 1. Berkeley: University of California Press, 1932.

O'Neill, (Mrs.) H.C. *Devonshire Idyls*. 7th ed. 1892; rpt. [London]: Andrew Melrose (1927), Ltd. n.d.

Paulme, Denise, ed. *Women of Tropical Africa*. Berkeley and Los Angeles: University of California Press, 1963.

Pearsall, Marion. *Little Smoky Ridge*. [University, Alabama]: University of Alabama Press, 1959.

Potter, Louisa. *Lancashire Memories*. London: Macmillan and Co., 1879.

Pruitt, Ida. *A Daughter of the Han: The Autobiography of a Chinese Working Woman*. New Haven, Conn.: Yale University Press, 1945.

Reichard, Gladys A. *Dezba: Woman of the Desert*. New York: J.J. Augustin, 1939.

Reichard, Gladys A. *Spider Woman: A Story of Navajo Weavers and Chanters*. New York: The Macmillan Company, 1934.

Richardson, (Mrs.) Ethel M. *Wiltshire Folk*. London: Heath Cranton Limited, 1934.

Ritchie, Jean. *Singing Family of the Cumberlands*. New York: Oxford University Press, 1955.

Robinson, Maude. *A South Down Farm in the Sixties*. London: J.M. Dent & Sons Ltd., 1938.

Russell, Laura. *Laura Russell Remembers*. Ed. Marion L. Channing. Marion, Mass.: Marion L. Channing, 1970.

Russell, Loris. *Everyday Life in Colonial Canada*. Toronto: Copp Clark Publishing Company, 1973.

Sayers, Peig. *An Old Woman's Reflections*. Trans. Séamus Ennis. London: Oxford University Press, 1962.

[Scherk, Michael Gonder]. *Pen Pictures of Early Pioneer Life in Upper Canada*. By a "Canuck" (of the fifth generation). 1905; rpt. Toronto: Coles Publishing Company, 1972.

Seabury, R.I. *Daughter of Africa*. Boston: Pilgrim Press, 1945.

Sneller, Anne Gertrude. *A Vanished World*. [Syracuse, N.Y.]: Syracuse Univ. Press, 1964.

Spindler, Louise S. *Menominee Women and Culture Change*. Memoir 91, The American Anthropological Association; *American Anthropologist*, 64, No. 1, Part 2, February, 1962.

Taylor, Helen V. *A Time to Recall*. New York: W.W. Norton & Company, Inc., 1963.

Taylor, Rosser Howard. *Carolina Crossroads. A Study of Rural Life at the End of the Horse-and-Buggy Era*. Murfreesboro, N.C.: Johnson Publishing Company, 1966.

*Them Days* (Box 939, Happy Valley, Labrador), 1, No. 1 (August 1975) — . A quarterly. Interviews with Labrador women included in each issue.

Thigpen, Julia Arledge. *Ninety and One Years*. [Picayune, Miss.: S.G. Thigpen, 1965].

Thomas, Kathleen. *Purse Barley. The Story of a Farm-house*. London: Westaway Books, 1951.

Thompson, Flora. *Still Glides the Stream*. London: Geoffrey Cumberlege, Oxford University Press, 1948.

Tirabutana, P. *A Simple One: The Story of a Siamese Girlhood*. Ithaca, N.Y.: Cornell University Press, 1958.

Treneer, Anne. *Cornish Years*. London: Jonathan Cape, 1949.

Treneer, Anne. *School House in the Wind*. 1944; rpt. London: Jonathan Cape, 1953.

Underhill, Ruth. *The Autobiography of a Papago Woman*. Memoirs of the American Anthropological Association, No. 46; Supplement to *American Anthropologist*, 38, No. 3, Part 2, 1936.

Uttley, Alison. *Ambush of Young Days*. 1937; rpt. London: Faber and Faber Limited, 1951.

Uttley, Alison. *Carts and Candlesticks*. London: Faber and Faber, 1948.

Uttley, Alison. *The Country Child*. 1931; rpt. London: Faber and Faber Limited, 1947.

Uttley, Alison. *Country Things*. London: Faber and Faber Limited, 1946.

Uttley, Alison. *The Farm on the Hill*. 1941; rpt. London: Faber and Faber Limited, 1949.

Vaughan, Eliza. *"The Stream of Time." Sketches of Village Life in Days Gone by*. Colchester: Benham & Company Limited, 1926.

Ward, Barbara E., ed. *Women in the New Asia*. Paris: UNESCO, 1963.

159

Washburne, Heluiz Chandler. *Land of the Good Shadows. The Life Story of Anauta, an Eskimo Woman.* New York: John Day Company, 1940.

Watkins, Floyd C. and Charles Hubert Watkins. *Yesterday in the Hills.* Chicago: Quadrangle Books, 1963.

West, James. [*pseudonym* for Carl Withers]. *Plainville, U.S.A.* New York: Columbia University Press, 1945.

Williams, Gertrude. *Women and Work.* London: Nicholson & Watson, 1945.

Wood, Frances Hariott. *Somerset Memories and Traditions.* London: Robert Scott, 1924.

Woodward, Marcus. *The Mistress of Stantons Farm.* London: Heath Cranton Limited, 1938.

Yetman, Norman R., ed. *Voices from Slavery.* 1970; rpt. New York: Holt, Rinehart and Winston, 1972.